Crowley - A
A Graphi<

C000258454

John S Moore
Illustrated by
John Patrick Higgins

Design and formatting by Alistair Moore

MANDRAKE

© John S Moore & John Patrick Higgins 2015

First Edition

Published by Mandrake

9781906958695

All rights reserved. No part of this work may be reproduced, stored in a retrieval system, or transmitted in any form or by any means, electronic, mechanical, photocopying, recording or otherwise without the prior permission of the publisher.

Contents

Introduction

The graphic guide is one of the success stories of recent years, introducing students to a range of thinkers and subjects, ancient and modern. Aleister Crowley is one of the hidden influences on our era. The full range of his achievement is little understood, and what is known is usually deplored. Crowley's life has great entertainment value, but he had a very serious side and was closely involved with many of the artistic and intellectual currents of his age. He was one of the most radical and interesting figures of the twentieth century, but reservations about the occult as well as the scandalous aspects of his life and personality have impeded the serious study he deserves. Writer John Moore and artist John Higgins have produced a lively and easy to follow introduction to this fascinating subject. It is hoped it will spark further interest in him.

Life

Edward Alexander Crowley, who later changed his first name to Aleister, was born 12th October 1875 into a wealthy brewing family. His father was a preacher in the extreme Protestant sect of the Plymouth Brethren who upheld a very literal interpretation of the Bible. His father died when he was 11. He was rude about his mother, whom he called...

...A BRAINLESS BIGOT OF THE MOST NARROW, LOGICAL, AND INHUMAN TYPE.

Nevertheless he was very upset when she died in 1917. The experiences of his childhood gave him a lasting hatred of Christianity.

BUT WHOSO SHALL OFFEND ONE OF THESE LITTLE ONES WHICH BELIEVE IN ME, IT WERE BETTER FOR HIM THAT A MILLSTONE WERE HANGED ABOUT HIS NECK, AND HE WERE DROWNED IN THE DEPTH OF THE SEA.

Decadence

He was up at Cambridge at the height of the decadent movement.
He wrote decadent poetry which he published out of his own pocket.
He met Aubrey Beardsley.

AUBREY ATTAINED IN SLEEP WHEN HE DREAMT THIS WONDERFUL DREAM OF WOMEN, TENDER CHILD...

AND HARLOT, NAKED ALL, IN THOUSANDS PILED ON ONE HOT WRITHING HEAP, HIS SHAMEFUL KISS...

An important theme of the movement was expressed in the French phrase "épater le bourgeois", meaning to shock the respectable middle classes.

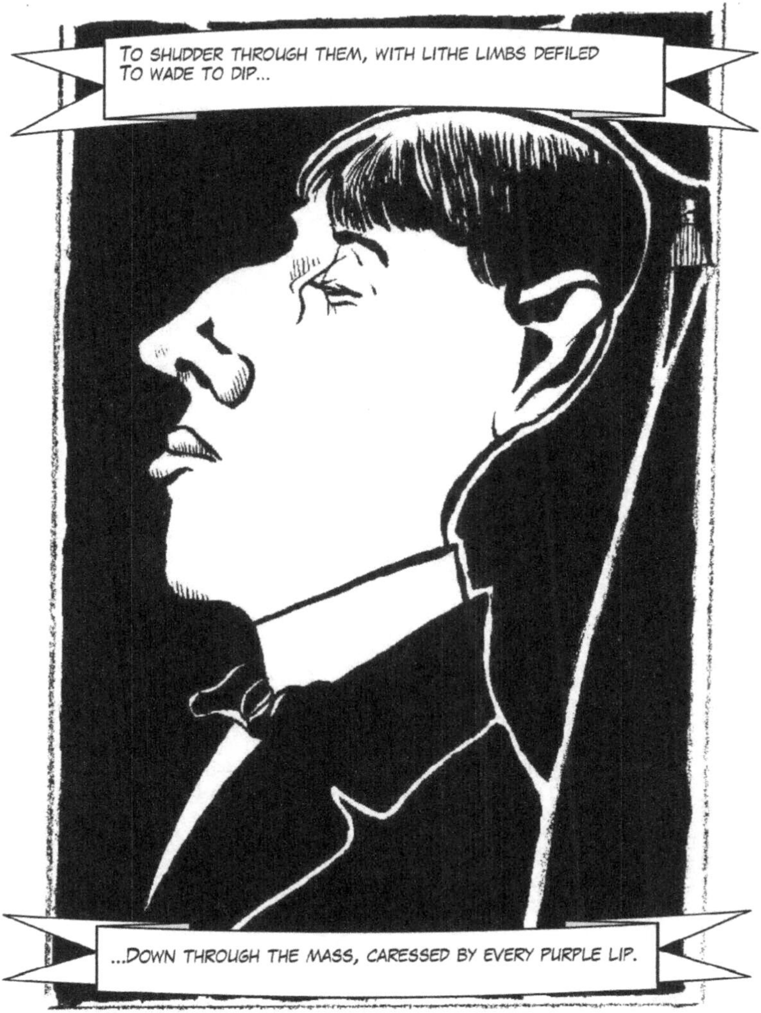
TO SHUDDER THROUGH THEM, WITH LITHE LIMBS DEFILED
TO WADE TO DIP...
...DOWN THROUGH THE MASS, CARESSED BY EVERY PURPLE LIP.

Romanticism

The decadent movement was a late form of romanticism. The search for hidden knowledge was one aspect of the romantic impulse.

Crowley admired Shelley and Byron and saw himself as continuing their tradition.

I WAS PASSIONATELY ENAMOURED OF THE VIEWS OF SHELLEY...

He shared Shelley's enthusiasm for the exotic and the occult, and took up the cause of anarchistic, antichristian rebellion.

I NEVER WAS ATTACHED TO THAT GREAT SECT,
WHOSE DOCTRINE IS, THAT EACH ONE SHOULD SELECT
OUT OF THE CROWD A MISTRESS OR A FRIEND,
AND ALL THE REST, THOUGH FAIR AND WISE, COMMEND
TO COLD OBLIVION, THOUGH IT IS IN THE CODE
OF MODERN MORALS, AND THE BEATEN ROAD
WHICH THOSE POOR SLAVES WITH WEARY FOOTSTEPS TREAD,
WHO TRAVEL TO THEIR HOME AMONG THE DEAD
BY THE BROAD HIGHWAY OF THE WORLD, AND SO
WITH ONE CHAINED FRIEND, PERHAPS A JEALOUS FOE,
THE DREARIEST AND THE LONGEST JOURNEY GO.

The Beast

As a naughty child he was called the Beast by his exasperated Bible reading mother. The Beast appears in the last book of the Christian Bible, the Revelation of St John the Divine, also known as the Apocalypse.

AND I STOOD UPON THE SAND OF THE SEA, AND SAW A BEAST RISE UP OUT OF THE SEA, HAVING SEVEN HEADS AND TEN HORNS, AND UPON HIS HORNS TEN CROWNS, AND UPON HIS HEADS THE NAME OF BLASPHEMY.

This was an identity which he eagerly embraced. His personality became dominated by and expressive of this identity. It relates to Nietzsche's idea of the Ubermensch.

...RATHER LOOK FOR A CESARE BORGIA THAN A PARSIFAL.

IN GREEK, TÒ ΜΕΓΑ ΘΗΡΊΟΝ ANGLICISED AS THE MASTER THERION.

This was part of his project for a religious reformation, abolishing Christianity and founding a new religion.

Absurd

Many consider it was absurd for him to call himself the Beast 666.

His Biographers

John Symonds was chosen by the old Crowley to be his biographer. Symonds lived to a great age and wrote several versions of Crowley's life making a good living out of it but turned steadily more against his subject, as, according to his obituaries, he grew steadily more right wing. An early version was published in paperback with a highly lurid cover and the blurb:

NO DEED WAS TOO HIDEOUS NO SIN TOO EVIL FOR... THE WICKEDEST MAN IN THE WORLD!

Charles Richard Cammell saw Crowley as a great poet, but deplored some aspects of his character. Susan Roberts gave a feminine perspective on the Beast.

Martin Booth shows how Crowley's puritanical upbringing gave an especial edge to pleasure. Francis King emphasised his sex magick and the religion of Thelema.

Israel Regardie worked as his secretary until Crowley offended him and they fell out badly. Many years later, objecting to Symonds' book he decided to set the record straight, as he saw it.

Lawrence Sutin deplored Crowley's racism and sexism. There are others...

Ambition

Crowley set out determined to enjoy his life and to exceed. One early ambition soon abandoned was to become a chess grandmaster.

Others were a scientist and a diplomat. Summarising his own achievements in later years he said:

HIS TIME HAS BEEN SPENT IN THREE VERY DISTINCT MANNERS: THE SECRET WAY OF THE INITIATE, THE PATH OF POETRY AND PHILOSOPHY, AND THE OPEN SEA OF ROMANCE AND ADVENTURE.

THE SECRET WAY OF THE INITIATE

THE PATH OF POETRY AND PHILOSOPHY

THE OPEN SEA OF ROMANCE AND ADVENTURE

Secret Path of the Initiate

In 1898 Crowley was initiated into the Hermetic order of the Golden Dawn, a Masonic style secret society with a number of distinguished Members including S L Mathers, W B Yeats, Algernon Blackwood, Bram Stoker, Florence Farr, Allan Bennett, and A E Waite.

The most important of these for his future development were Mathers and Bennett.

Samuel Liddell 'Macgregor' Mathers (1854-1918) was a highly eccentric and original occultist, aspects of whose flamboyant persona Crowley has been accused of blatantly copying. He translated a number of ancient magical books, so introducing them to a non academic public.

Allan Bennett (1872 - 1923) personally tutored Crowley in Magic.

He later travelled to the east with Crowley's financial assistance where he studied yoga, then became a Buddhist monk in Burma, and later a Buddhist missionary to the west.

The Golden Dawn practiced ritual magic.

Crowley took the name Perdurabo, which means in Latin 'I will endure unto the end'.

Grades

The initiation system of the Golden Dawn was to remain the framework on which he would hang much of his thought.

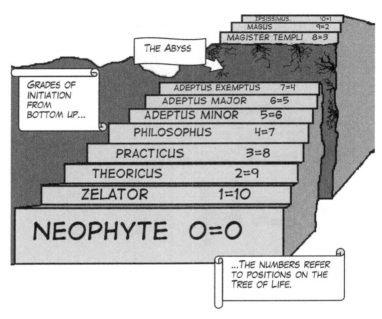

THE ABYSS

IPSISSIMUS.	10=1	
MAGUS	9=2	
MAGISTER TEMPLI	8=3	

GRADES OF INITIATION FROM BOTTOM UP...

ADEPTUS EXEMPTUS	7=4
ADEPTUS MAJOR	6=5
ADEPTUS MINOR	5=6
PHILOSOPHUS	4=7
PRACTICUS	3=8
THEORICUS	2=9
ZELATOR	1=10
NEOPHYTE	0=0

...THE NUMBERS REFER TO POSITIONS ON THE TREE OF LIFE.

As a member of the Golden Dawn Crowley had rapidly advanced through the lower stages.

Strictly speaking the Golden Dawn was the outer order of the Great White Brotherhood, up to the grade of Philosophus. The next three grades were the Rosicrucian Order of the Red Rose and the Golden Cross. Beyond the Abyss were the grades of the Secret Chiefs in the Argenteum Astrum.

It has been suggested we understand the crossing of Abyss as essentially a projection of Crowley's own personal crisis.

His *Book of Lies* was written for the Babes of the Abyss.

In 1921 he took the oath of Ipsissimus, initiating himself into the highest possible grade, beyond all the gods.

The Abyss

The Abyss was situated between the grades of Adeptus Exemptus and Master of the Temple. Crossing the Abyss was what Crowley identified as the greatest spiritual/psychological crisis of his life.

...TO THE MAN WHO HAS NOT PASSED ENTIRELY THROUGH THE ABYSS THOUGHTS OF THIS KIND ARE POSITIVELY FRIGHTFUL. THERE IS NO RATIONAL ANSWER POSSIBLE, FROM THE NATURE OF THE CASE; AND I WAS TORMENTED INDESCRIBABLY BY THESE THOUGHTS, THOUSANDS AFTER THOUSANDS, EACH A TERRIFIC THUNDERBOLT BLASTING ITS WAY THROUGH MY BRAIN DURING THESE FRIGHTFUL MONTHS.

EVENTUALLY HE MANAGED: THE ACT OF VIRILE ASSERTION WHICH IS THE ONLY WAY OF OVERCOMING THE HORRORS AND CONTRADICTIONS OF THE ABYSS.

For Crowley this experience was not to be confused with "elementary mysticism in all its branches" when...

...ONE TAKES A LIVELY INTEREST IN THE WORK; IT SEEMS EASY; ONE IS QUITE PLEASED TO HAVE STARTED. THIS STAGE REPRESENTS ISIS. SOONER OR LATER IT IS SUCCEEDED BY DEPRESSION - THE DARK NIGHT OF THE SOUL, AN INFINITE WEARINESS AND DETESTATION OF THE WORK...

...THE SIMPLEST AND EASIEST ACTS BECOME ALMOST IMPOSSIBLE TO PERFORM. SUCH IMPOTENCE FILLS THE MIND WITH APPREHENSION AND DESPAIR. THE INTENSITY OF THIS LOATHING CAN HARDLY BE UNDERSTOOD BY ANY PERSON WHO HAS NOT EXPERIENCED IT. THIS IS THE PERIOD OF APOPHIS.

The conception of the Abyss belonged to a much higher plane.

DESOLATION IS A FILE, AND THE ENDURANCE OF DARKNESS IS PREPARATION FOR GREAT LIGHT.

Nevertheless the Abyss has been compared to the **Dark Night of the Soul** of Christian mystics like St John of the Cross.

The Path of Poetry

He continued to write poetry all his life. Some thought it wonderful, others execrable.

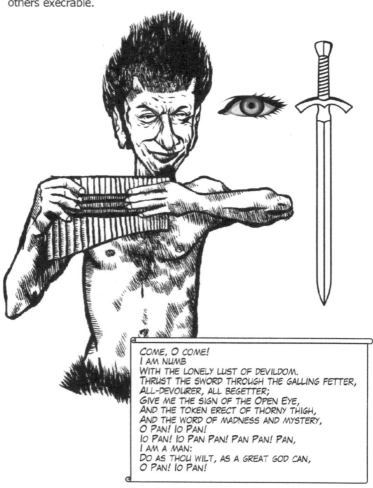

COME, O COME!
I AM NUMB
WITH THE LONELY LUST OF DEVILDOM.
THRUST THE SWORD THROUGH THE GALLING FETTER,
ALL-DEVOURER, ALL BEGETTER;
GIVE ME THE SIGN OF THE OPEN EYE,
AND THE TOKEN ERECT OF THORNY THIGH,
AND THE WORD OF MADNESS AND MYSTERY,
O PAN! IO PAN!
IO PAN! IO PAN PAN! PAN PAN! PAN,
I AM A MAN:
DO AS THOU WILT, AS A GREAT GOD CAN,
O PAN! IO PAN!

Open Sea of Romance

Towards the end of his life, he refers to Cardinal Newman (whom he mostly despised):

Open Sea of Adventure

The Victorian explorer and orientalist Sir Richard Burton was one of his heroes. Burton had travelled to Mecca in disguise and around the lakes of East Africa in search of the source of the Nile.

He translated oriental classics like the *Arabian Nights*, the *Kama Sutra* and *The Perfumed Garden Of The Shaykh Nefzawi*, as well as writing stories and poems of his own, notably *The Kasidah*, a long poem of Sufi style philosophy which strongly influenced Crowley.

CROWLEY AIMED TO DO FOR THE SPIRITUAL WHAT BURTON HAD DONE FOR THE GEOGRAPHICAL...

...NEVERTHELESS HE ALSO EXPLORED GEOGRAPHICALLY.

HE TRAVELLED EXTENSIVELY, CROSSED DESERTS AND CLIMBED MOUNTAINS...

FOR A WHILE, HE HELD A NUMBER OF RECORDS.

...HIS EXPEDITION TO KANCHENJUNGA IN THE HIMALAYAS ENDED IN DISASTER AND RECRIMINATION.

The Path of Philosophy

Crowley advocates the study of all philosophy, sceptical as well as mystical. He did not tie himself down to any one theory or school.

HE SOUGHT A POSITION ABOVE ALL RIVALRY BETWEEN PHILOSOPHERS.

BUT ALSO HE GETS TO RAISE SOME DEEP PHILOSOPHICAL ISSUES, SUCH AS THOSE ARISING WHEN CONFRONTED WITH THE CONFUSION OF THE ABYSS.

Nietzsche

His strongest philosophical influence was the nineteenth century German Friedrich Nietzsche.

NIETZSCHE WAS TO ME ALMOST AN AVATAR OF THOTH, THE GOD OF WISDOM...

GOD IS DEAD

THE ÜBERMENSCH

TRANSVALUATION OF ALL VALUES

THE WORLD IS WILL TO POWER AND NOTHING BESIDES

I CALL PAGAN EVERYTHING THAT SAYS YES TO LIFE

I WISH TO BE ANYTIME HEREAFTER ONLY A YEA SAYER!

Understanding his Nietzscheanism is the key to taking him seriously. In his personal life Nietzsche did not match up to his own philosophy. Arguably Crowley did.

Mountaineering

Nietzsche influenced twentieth century mountaineering. He walked in the Alps. Crowley broke altitude records in the Himalayas.

Affirmation

Crowley produced a form of Nietzschean theosophy. He put Nietzscheanism into living practice as well as tapping the spiritual heritage of the entire human race.

THE BRAVE MAN REJOICES IN GIVING AND TAKNG HARD KNOCKS, AND THE BRAVE MAN IS JOYOUS... HE UNDERSTANDS THAT THE ONLY JOY WORTH WHILE IS THE JOY OF CONTINUAL VICTORY, AND VICTORY ITSELF WOULD BECOME AS TAME AS CROQUET IF IT WERE NOT SPICED BY EQUALLY CONTINUAL DEFEAT.

Like the Marquis de Sade, Crowley held it was possible to enjoy and affirm even the seemingly worst fates.

If you are sentenced to death, he says, once you have passed through the fear and horror you will find that being executed is a joyous experience.

Balance

Even Nietzsche, though, was subject to Magickal balance.

BALANCE EVERY THOUGHT WITH ITS OPPOSITION. BECAUSE THE MARRIAGE OF THEM IS THE DESTRUCTION OF ILLUSION.

IT IS NOT SAFE TO USE ANY THOUGHT IN MAGICK UNLESS THAT THOUGHT HAS BEEN EQUILIBRATED AND DESTROYED.

A principle Crowley discovered in the Kabbalah.

Dress

Crowley would not have agreed with Nietzsche that a concern with personal display is incompatible with true seriousness.

His impatience of conventional limits extended to his dress.

Variously he appeared in public as a highland chieftain, in pink tights, and as an oriental prince.

He wore exotic rings on his fingers and covered himself with a strange smelling unguent.

Identity

Crowley also adopted a number of exotic names and titles.

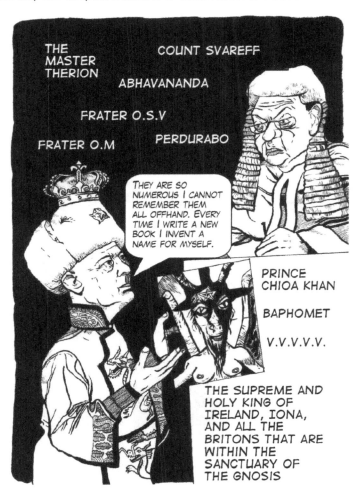

THE MASTER THERION

COUNT SVAREFF

ABHAVANANDA

FRATER O.S.V

FRATER O.M

PERDURABO

THEY ARE SO NUMEROUS I CANNOT REMEMBER THEM ALL OFFHAND. EVERY TIME I WRITE A NEW BOOK I INVENT A NAME FOR MYSELF.

PRINCE CHIOA KHAN

BAPHOMET

V.V.V.V.V.

THE SUPREME AND HOLY KING OF IRELAND, IONA, AND ALL THE BRITONS THAT ARE WITHIN THE SANCTUARY OF THE GNOSIS

Espionage

He wrote over the top propaganda from America for Germany in the First World War. For that he would seem to have been a simple traitor, but there is some (inconclusive) evidence he was working for the British Secret Service throughout his life. Typically there was ambiguity between traitor and patriot.

Theosophy

Theosophy is the ancient idea of a common esoteric truth behind all religions. The modern Theosophical Society was founded by Mme Blavatsky, in 1875, the year of Crowley's birth (a significant coincidence according to Crowley).

In this spirit Crowley made a serious study of oriental traditions.

Useful Myths

For the Golden Dawn Blavatsky's Hidden Masters became Secret Chiefs. The idea is traceable back to the Rosicrucians. Crowley adopted this mythology. Eventually he counted himself as one of their company.

THE SECRET DOCTRINE IS THE COMMON PROPERTY OF THE COUNTLESS MILLIONS OF MEN BORN UNDER VARIOUS CLIMATES, IN TIMES WITH WHICH HISTORY REFUSES TO DEAL, AND TO WHICH ESOTERIC TEACHINGS ASSIGN DATES INCOMPATIBLE WITH THE THEORIES OF GEOLOGY AND ANTHROPOLOGY.

"...THE SECRET CHIEFS WERE DETERMINED NOT TO ALLOW ME TO FOOL MYSELF. WHEN THEY PICKED ME OUT TO DO THEIR WORK THEY MEANT ME TO GET BUSY AND DO IT, AND WERE GOING TO SEE THAT I DID."

Rosicrucians

These are central to the western esoteric tradition as it developed over the past few centuries. The Rosicrucians were a legendary secret society of initiated sages allegedly founded by Christian Rosenkreuz in 1407. Two hundred years later two manifestos were published announcing a general reform of civilisation and culture on a basis of esoteric wisdom. They created a stir.

Rosicrucianism had a seminal influence on Freemasonry, and of course the Golden Dawn. Edward Bulwer-Lytton's *Zanoni* is subtitled *A Rosicrucian Tale*.

In 1917 Crowley's poem *The Rose and the Cross* was published in *The Oxford Book of English Mystical Verse*.

THE ROSY CROSS, SYMBOL OF THE ROSICRUCIANS.

ITS MYRIAD PETALS OF DIVIDED LIGHT;

ITS LEAVES OF THE MOST RADIANT EMERALD;

ITS HEART OF FIRE LIKE RUBIES. AT THE SIGHT I LIFTED UP MY HEART TO GOD AND CALLED:

HOW SHALL I PLUCK THIS DREAM OF MY DESIRE?

AND LO! THERE SHAPED ITSELF THE CROSS OF FIRE!

Orientalism

Crowley also admired eastern esoteric traditions. Such an interest has been denounced as Orientalism. Recently Edward Said, founder of post colonial studies, has led the attack.

MY CONTENTION IS THAT ORIENTALISM IS FUNDAMENTALLY A POLITICAL DOCTRINE WILLED OVER THE ORIENT BECAUSE THE ORIENT WAS WEAKER THAN THE WEST, WHICH ELIDED THE ORIENT'S DIFFERENCE WITH ITS WEAKNESS...

...AS A CULTURAL APPARATUS ORIENTALISM IS ALL AGGRESSION, ACTIVITY, JUDGMENT, WILL-TO-TRUTH, AND KNOWLEDGE. (ORIENTALISM, *P.204*).

Imperialism

Crowley would presumably have been unfazed.

Aiwass was an imperialist.

> I AM UNIQUE & CONQUEROR. I AM NOT OF THE SLAVES THAT PERISH. BE THEY DAMNED & DEAD! BUT THE KEEN AND THE PROUD, THE ROYAL AND THE LOFTY; YE ARE BROTHERS! AS BROTHERS FIGHT YE!

Crowley supported the British Empire but foresaw its decline. At the height of imperial power, he wrote that:

...THE ENGLISHMAN LIVES ON THE EXCREMENT OF HIS FOREFATHERS.

Pranks

Crowley was a great practical joker and prankster; Sculptor Jacob Epstein's monument for the Oscar Wilde tomb in the Pere Lachaise cemetery was judged indecent by the Parisian authorities so a big brass butterfly was placed over the penis. Crowley stole this, took it to London, and walked into the Café Royal with it covering his fly. Epstein was present and much amused.

TRANSCEND, O MAGE, THY SOUL REDEEMED!
HER MERCY SHONE WHERE SORROW STEAMED.
EXALTED IN THE SKIES OF EVEN
VIRTUE HATH CLEARED THY WAY TO HEAVEN.
IN DARKNESS HIDES THE GLITTERING ORE.
REVEALED THY LIGHT, O MYSTIC LORE
GIVEN BY GOD, LEST I SHOULD ERR
IN DEXTER OR IN SINISTER.
NOW MARY VIRGIN TO MY SPEECH
MARRIED HER FIRE THAT ALL AND EACH
AT LAST SHOULD GATHER TO THE TRYST
RIPE SUNS ARISEN ABOVE THE MIDST!
YEA! THOU HAST GIVEN ME FAVOUR! YEA!
IN UTMOST LOVE AND AWE WE PRAY;
DEVOTED TO THY REVERENCE.
ENKINDLE I THE SWEET INCENSE.
SECURE FROM ALL THE FEARS THAT CHILL
IN PEACE FROM THEM THAT RAGE AND KILL;
RECEIVE, O QUEEN, THE GLAD ORATION
EVEN FROM A LOST AND PAGAN NATION.
BUT THOU WILL MAKE US WHOLLY FIT
UNTO THY GRACE AND CARE OF IT.
TILL ALL THE ELIXIR DO RECEIVE
(AMEN) TO HEAL THE HURT OF EVE.

He published poems in religious journals with obscene and blasphemous messages hidden in the text.

42

Lumber of the Centuries

Untrue Legends

Crowley inspired a large number of colourful false stories. Here are a few:

WHILE HE WAS AT CAMBRIDGE UNDERGRADUATE 'HEARTIES' THREW HIM IN A FOUNTAIN FOR BEING 'DIRTY INSIDE AND OUT'.

HE WAS A CANNIBAL.

AS A GUEST HE USED TO DEFECATE ON PEOPLES' LIVING ROOM FLOORS AND ANNOUNCE HIS EXCRETA WAS SACRED.

HE SACRIFICED CHILDREN.

HE CHANGED VICTOR NEUBURG INTO A CAMEL AND SOLD HIM TO THE ZOO IN ALEXANDRIA.

Yoga

Crowley wrote *Eight Lectures on Yoga* (originally entitled *Yoga for Yahoos.*) He studied Yoga and Buddhism in Ceylon under the tutelage of Allan Bennett who had learned from oriental masters. Eventually he achieved (or so he claimed) Samadhi, the supreme goal of Yoga.

...THAT STATE OF MIND IN WHICH SUBJECT AND OBJECT, BECOMING ONE, HAVE DISAPPEARED.

He devised yogic style disciplines for his pupils.

WHEN YOU HAVE PROGRESSED UP TO THE POINT THAT A SAUCER FILLED TO THE BRIM WITH WATER AND POISED UPON THE HEAD DOES NOT SPILL ONE DROP DURING A WHOLE HOUR, AND WHEN YOU CAN NO LONGER PERCEIVE THE SLIGHTEST TREMOR IN ANY MUSCLE; WHEN, IN SHORT, YOU ARE PERFECTLY STEADY AND EASY, YOU WILL BE ADMITTED FOR EXAMINATION; AND, SHOULD YOU PASS, YOU WILL BE INSTRUCTED IN MORE COMPLEX AND DIFFICULT PRACTICES.

Hoax

WITH ASSISTANCE OF PORTUGUESE POET FERNANDO PESSOA HE STAGED HIS OWN DEATH BY DROWNING IN 1933.

Pessoa himself is critically acclaimed as one of the greatest poets of the twentieth century. He translated the *Hymn to Pan* into Portuguese, possessed copies of *Magick in Theory and Practice* and the *Confessions*, and was strongly influenced by Crowley in his own creative thought. Like Crowley he developed multiple identities.

Iô Pã! Iô Pã! Do mar de além
Vem da Sicília e da Arcádia vem!
Vem como Baco, com fauno e fera
E ninfa e sátiro à tua beira,
Num asno lácteo, do mar sem fim,
A mim, a mim!
Vem com Apolo, nupcial na brisa
(Pegureira e pitonisa),
Vem com Artêmis, leve e estranha,
E a coxa branca, Deus lindo, banha
Ao luar do bosque, em marmóreo monte,
Manhã malhada da âmbrea fonte!

Astrology

His astrological writings make a 230 page book. Yet he said to his biographer:

I THINK THAT THERE IS ONLY A FRACTION OF ONE PERCENT OF TRUTH IN ASTROLOGY.

As in other occult sciences, he made his own original contributions. Here's one from his Magical Diary for 21st November 1914:

> IF THERE BE ANY TRUTH IN ASTROLOGY, SURELY THE MOMENT OF THE BIRTH OF THE ELIXIR ꞊SEMEN꞊ SHOULD DETERMINE ITS CAREER. THEREFORE LET ME INVARIABLY ERECT A FIGURE GENETHLIACAL FOR THE Λογος OR SEMEN AT THE MOMENT OF ITS CREATION FROM THE ELEMENTS THAT COMPOSE IT.

Kabbalah

This was Jewish mysticism that has often been appropriated and reinterpreted by gentiles. Crowley developed his own system, to be found especially in:

Book 777 - a table of correspondences.

The Book of Lies - of which he was most proud.

The Book of Thoth - tarot cards with kabbalistic correspondences.

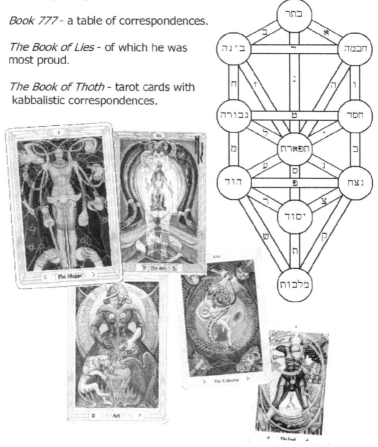

Tree of Life

The initiated interpretation of the Jewish scriptures. Mostly either unintelligible or nonsense, he says in *Little Essays towards Truth*.

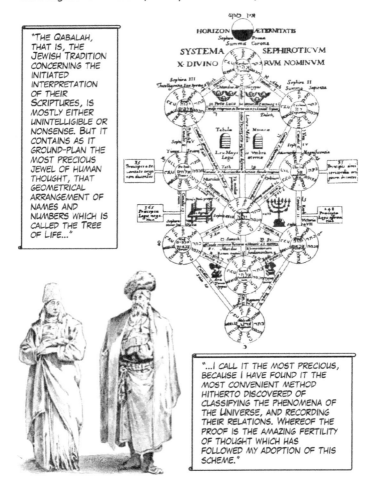

"THE QABALAH, THAT IS, THE JEWISH TRADITION CONCERNING THE INITIATED INTERPRETATION OF THEIR SCRIPTURES, IS MOSTLY EITHER UNINTELLIGIBLE OR NONSENSE. BUT IT CONTAINS AS IT GROUND-PLAN THE MOST PRECIOUS JEWEL OF HUMAN THOUGHT, THAT GEOMETRICAL ARRANGEMENT OF NAMES AND NUMBERS WHICH IS CALLED THE TREE OF LIFE..."

"...I CALL IT THE MOST PRECIOUS, BECAUSE I HAVE FOUND IT THE MOST CONVENIENT METHOD HITHERTO DISCOVERED OF CLASSIFYING THE PHENOMENA OF THE UNIVERSE, AND RECORDING THEIR RELATIONS. WHEREOF THE PROOF IS THE AMAZING FERTILITY OF THOUGHT WHICH HAS FOLLOWED MY ADOPTION OF THIS SCHEME."

I Ching

He used this regularly for divination, and based decisions upon it. He saw it as essentially the same as the Kabbalah but based on the binary rather than the decimal system. The similarity, he says, confirms the truth of both.

He produced his own translation.

Tantrism

This is a form of Hinduism spoken of as the left hand path, notable for its sexuality, drug use and taboo breaking.

INDEED, AT THIS DAY THERE ARE MANY CULTS IN INDIA OF WHAT IS CALLED THE VAMACHARYA. RELIGIOUS FRENZY IS INVOKED BY THE AID TO THE EROTIC AND BACCHIC FRENZIES MINGLED WITH THAT OF THE MUSE OF THE TOM-TOM, SOMA, BHANG, ARRAQ, AND THE UNITING OF THE LINGAM AND THE YONI! ALL, MIND YOU, BY A MOST ELABORATE RITUAL.

Gnosticism

Much in the old heresies grouped as Gnosticism, with their dismissal of the God of the Jews and Christians as an evil demiurge, was congenial to Crowley.

IT APPEARS THAT THE LEVANT, FROM BYZANTIUM AND ATHENS TO DAMASCUS, JERUSALEM, ALEXANDRIA AND CAIRO, WAS PREOCCUPIED WITH THE FORMULATION OF THIS ⸗WHITE⸗ SCHOOL IN A POPULAR RELIGION, BEGINNING IN THE DAYS OF AUGUSTUS CAESAR. FOR THERE ARE ELEMENTS OF THIS CENTRAL IDEA IN THE WORKS OF THE GNOSTICS... THE DOCTRINE BECAME ABOMINABLY CORRUPTED IN COMMITTEE, SO TO SPEAK, AND THE RESULT WAS CHRISTIANITY...

Fig. 3.

...THE CADUCEUS CONTAINS A COMPLETE SYMBOL OF THE GNOSIS: THE WINGED SUN OR PHALLUS REPRESENTS THE JOY OF LIFE ON ALL PLACES FROM THE LOWEST TO THE HIGHEST. THE SERPENTS, BESIDES BEING ACTIVE AND PASSIVE, HORUS AND OSIRIS, AND ALL THEIR OTHER WELL-KNOWN ATTRIBUTIONS ARE THOSE QUALITIES OF EAGLE AND LION RESPECTIVELY, OF WHICH WE KNOW BUT DO NOT SPEAK.

Biblical Exegesis

There were Gnostic schools that took the side of the enemies of the God of the Old Testament: Cain, the Sodomites, the Serpent in the Garden of Eden, etc.

This fitted in well with the sympathies Crowley had had since a child. Jezebel was his favourite female character.

"Now let me die, to mix my soul
With thy red soul, to join our hands
To weld us in one perfect whole
To link us with desirous bands
Now let me die, to mate in hell
With thee, O Harlot Jezebel."

According to the central Gnostic myth of Ialdabaoth, into which Crowley bought, the forces of unenlightenment are represented by the God of the orthodox, renamed Ialdabaoth.

He falsely and ignorantly claims to be the one true God. In reality he is the demiurge who works to keep man away from the light.

Alchemy

Most alchemical texts are unintelligible, Crowley tells us. Nonetheless he derives great inspiration from the alchemical concept of the Great Work which is an invaluable metaphor for the development and attainment of the true will, a lifetime project different from the otherworldly enlightenment sought by the mystic.

In 15th century Europe alchemy informed political as well as psychological thinking. In more modern times both Carl Jung and Wolfgang von Goethe found a use for alchemical ideas.

Phallicism

Crowley's religion was strongly influenced by the eighteenth century anthropology of Richard Payne Knight who wrote *An Account of the Remains of the Worship of Priapus.*

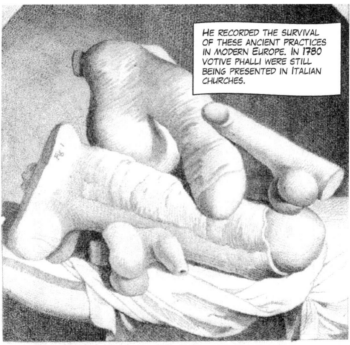

HE RECORDED THE SURVIVAL OF THESE ANCIENT PRACTICES IN MODERN EUROPE. IN 1780 VOTIVE PHALLI WERE STILL BEING PRESENTED IN ITALIAN CHURCHES.

Ex Voto of Wax presented in the Church at Isernia 1780

Going further than Freud and Jung in the twentieth century, Knight effectively created a new religion, based on interpretations of the mysteries and symbols as they appear on coins and medals. For him Priapus was originally the ultimate reality. He viewed the neoplatonic 'One' as an abstracting reinterpretation of this elemental religion.

Identifying Christ himself with Priapus, he interpreted the Cross as a phallus. 'Priapus' Knight was inevitably accused of blasphemy and irreligion but he was one of the leading intellectuals of his own time.

Fig. 4

Crowley's religion, too, was solar-phallic. He wrote hymns to the sun and his 'viceregent'- meaning the phallus.

Fig. 3.

"NOT ONLY HAS CROWLEY SUCCEEDED IN FINDING ALL THE SCATTERED PIECES OF OSIRIS WHICH ISIS DISCOVERED, BUT ALSO HIS PHALLUS, WHICH SHE COULD NOT FIND." (J F C FULLER)

Hargrave Jennings

A book by Hargrave Jennings *The Rosicrucians: Their Rites and Mysteries* (1870) continued with the phallicist understanding of esoteric culture.

Placing the Arthurian legends side by side with contemporary *Roman de La Rose*, he showed the sexual character of the grail legend, as well as that of later Rosicrucianism.

Crowley followed this interpretation, writing of

...THE REAL CHASTITY OF PERCIVALE OR PARSIFAL, A CHASTITY WHICH DID NOT PREVENT HIS DIPPING THE POINT OF THE SACRED LANCE INTO THE HOLY GRAIL.

Jennings explained how the Order of the Garter was not really about a garter but a dropped sanitary towel.

The rose and the cross of the Rosicrucians were really the penis and the vagina.

Themes that continue in alchemy.

Contemporary critics noted an 'unwholesome current' of indecent innuendo throughout his book, but it was very influential in Victorian occult circles.

...NO BETTER BOOK UPON SUCH A THEME HAS BEEN WRITTEN, OR INDEED COULD BE WRITTEN UNLESS A MEMBER OF THE FRATERNITY WERE TO BREAK THE VOW WHICH ENJOINS HIM TO SECRECY...

E. BULWER-LYTTON

Madame Blavatsky wrote a pamphlet against phallicism, which she saw as an effort to undermine theosophy.

Holy Guardian Angel

A significant part of his occult synthesis was the project of attaining the knowledge and conversation of one's Holy Guardian Angel as described in *The Book of Sacred Magic of Abra Melin the Mage.*

When Crowley eventually did this he discovered that his was named Aiwass. This was the intelligence that dictated to him *The Book of the Law.*

HE WAS THE INTELLIGIBLE MEDIUM BETWEEN THE BABE GOD -- THE NEW AEON ABOUT TO BE BORN -- AND MYSELF. THIS BOOK OF THE LAW IS THE VOICE OF HIS MOTHER, HIS FATHER, AND HIMSELF. BUT ON HIS APPEARING, HE ASSUMES THE ACTIVE FORM TWIN TO HARPOCRATES, THAT OF RA-HOOR-KHUIT. THE CONCEALED CHILD BECOMES THE CONQUERING CHILD, THE ARMED HORUS.

Was Aiwass one of the Secret Chiefs, a deceiving demon, or Crowley's Higher Self? Or all three?

The Book of the Law

This was a three part poem received as a revelation over three nights in Cairo in 1904 while travelling with his first wife Rose.

> DO WHAT THOU WILT SHALL BE THE WHOLE OF THE LAW
> LOVE IS THE LAW LOVE UNDER WILL
> EVERY MAN AND EVERY WOMAN IS A STAR.
> LET MY SERVANTS BE FEW & SECRET:
> THOU HAS NO RIGHT BUT TO DO THY WILL.

He was the prophet of the new age of Horus, the crowned and conquering child. For Crowley it was far more than a poem. He later identified it as the scripture of a new religion.

THE AGE OF HORUS

Preceding eras

ISIS (MATRTIARCHY)

OSIRIS (THE DYING GOD)

Future era

MAAT (JUSTICE)

Thelema

Thelema (Θέλημα) is a Greek word meaning will. Thelemism was the doctrine propounded in *The Book of the Law*. The word was used by Rabelais for his fictional Abbey of Theleme.

There were thelemites before Crowley.

Crowley was concerned with the discovery of the 'true will' which is something different from simple desire. It suggests Heidegger's 'resolution'.

Sir Francis Dashwood founded his Monks of Medmenham on the principles of Rabelais' Abbey. This was popularly known as the Hell Fire Club.

Horus

He is the hawk headed god of the ancient Egyptians. He avenged the death of his father Osiris. His mother, Isis, conceived him after his father's death, resurrecting Osiris for the act.

In the great battle with his father's slayer Horus emerged victorious. With the closing of the era of the dying and resurrected god, represented most prominently, by Christianity, begins the new era, that of Horus, the crowned and conquering child, in which thelemic rather than Christian values will predominate.

ISIS

OSIRIS

Note that Dashwood's secret society venerated the image of Harpocrates, god of silence, one of the forms of Horus, who is also present in *The Book of the Law* but naturally says nothing.

HORUS

62

Blasphemy

"WITH MY HAWK'S HEAD I PECK AT THE EYES OF JESUS AS HE HANGS UPON THE CROSS.

I FLAP MY WINGS IN THE FACE OF MOHAMMED & BLIND HIM.

WITH MY CLAWS I TEAR OUT THE FLESH OF THE INDIAN AND THE BUDDHIST, MONGOL AND DIN.

BAHLASTI! OMPEHDA! I SPIT ON YOUR CRAPULOUS CREEDS." *(LIBER LEGIS 51-54)*

Crowley justified blasphemy theologically.

THE MAN WHO MAKES IDIOTIC JOKES AND DEVISES OBSCENE CRUELTIES PROVES HIMSELF OF THE SEED OF THE GOD WHO FILLED THE UNIVERSE WITH THESE FORMS OF AMUSEMENTS. AND "BLASPHEMY", WHICH IS THE INDIGNATION OF THE CREATED AT HIS CREATOR, IS THE PROOF THAT THE CREATED IS A LIVE AND INDEPENDENT BEING, FULFILLING THE TRUE PURPOSE OF THAT CREATOR. THEREFORE, OF ALL ACTS, BLASPHEMY IS THE MOST PLEASING TO GOD.

Wasteland

The Wasteland features in the Arthurian legends about the Holy Grail. Crowley made a pen and ink drawing of the entrance to the Wasteland.

As a poem *The Book of the Law* contrasts with T S Eliot's *Wasteland.*

Both expressed the zeitgeist. Eliot wrote shortly after the First World War, a poem full of disillusion and occult imagery, strongly influenced by Sir James Frazer's *Golden Bough.*

...MADAME SOSOSTRIS, FAMOUS CLAIRVOYANTE, HAD A BAD COLD, NEVERTHELESS IS KNOWN TO BE THE WISEST WOMAN IN EUROPE, WITH A WICKED PACK OF CARDS. HERE, SAID SHE, IS YOUR CARD, THE DROWNED PHOENICIAN SAILOR...

Crowley's was written ten years before the war, which Crowley claimed it prophesied. Its warlike imagery prefigured an increasingly aggressive and violent era.

The Book of the Law came to serve as the fundamental reference point for him. Its philosophy is thoroughly Nietzschean. The same goes for the other books of Thelema, the *Holy Books*.

"I AM THE WARRIOR LORD OF THE FORTIES: THE EIGHTIES COWER BEFORE ME, & ARE ABASED. I WILL BRING YOU TO VICTORY & JOY: I WILL BE AT YOUR ARMS IN BATTLE & YE SHALL DELIGHT TO SLAY. SUCCESS IS YOUR PROOF; COURAGE IS YOUR ARMOUR; GO ON, GO ON, IN MY STRENGTH; & YE SHALL TURN NOT BACK FOR ANY!"

He came to see those three days in 1904 as the focal point of his entire life.

Three Schools

He writes of three schools of magick; White, yellow and black.

The white is life affirming, the black life negating, and the yellow neutral. He says himself:

...THE PUREST DOCUMENTS OF THE WHITE SCHOOL ARE FOUND IN THE SACRED BOOKS OF THELEMA. THE CULMINATION OF THE BLACK PHILOSOPHY IS ONLY FOUND IN SCHOPENHAUER, AND WE MAY REGARD HIM AS HAVING BEEN OBSESSED, ON THE ONE HAND, BY THE DESPAIR BORN OF THAT FALSE SCEPTICISM WHICH HE LEARNT FROM THE BANKRUPTCY OF HUME AND KANT; ON THE OTHER, BY THE DIRECT OBSESSION OF THE BUDDHIST DOCUMENTS TO WHICH HE WAS ONE OF THE EARLIEST EUROPEANS TO OBTAIN ACCESS. (MAGICK WITHOUT TEARS 77-8)

...EXISTENCE IS PURE JOY. SORROW IS CAUSED BY FAILURE TO PERCEIVE THIS FACT; BUT THIS IS NOT A MISFORTUNE. WE HAVE INVENTED SORROW, WHICH DOES NOT MATTER SO MUCH AFTER ALL, IN ORDER TO HAVE THE EXUBERANT SATISFACTION OF GETTING RID OF IT.

IT IS A CLEAR GAIN TO SACRIFICE PLEASURE IN ORDER TO AVOID PAIN.

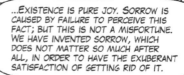

SCHOPENHAUER

Yellow

Yellow magick he associated with the Tao te Ching – an ancient Chinese philosophical poem of which he offered his own translation.

THE TAO TEH KING (LIBER CLVII)

A NEW TRANSLATION BY:

KO YUEN (ALEISTER CROWLEY)
THE EQUINOX (VOLUME III, NO. VIII)

1. IF WE FORGOT OUR STATESMANSHIP AND OUR WISDOM, IT WOULD BE AN HUNDRED TIMES BETTER FOR THE PEOPLE. IF WE FORGOT OUR BENEVOLENCE AND OUR JUSTICE, THEY WOULD BECOME AGAIN LIKE SONS, FOLK OF GOOD WILL. IF WE FORGET OUR MACHINES AND OUR BUSINESS, THERE WOULD BE NO KNAVERY.

2. THESE NEW METHODS DESPISED THE OLDEN WAY, INVENTING FINE NAMES TO DISGUISE THEIR BANENESS. BUT SIMPLICITY IN THE DOING OF THE WILL OF EVERY MAN WOULD PUT AN END TO VAIN AMBITIONS AND DESIRES. {CHAPTER XIX}

Magick

Crowley added the K to the word to distinguish what he was talking about from mere conjuring.

> THE SCIENCE AND ART OF CAUSING CHANGE TO OCCUR IN CONFORMITY WITH THE WILL.

He expanded the concepts of the anthropologist Sir James Frazer.

> SO FAR, THEREFORE, AS THE PUBLIC PROFESSION OF MAGIC HAS BEEN ONE OF THE ROADS BY WHICH THE ABLEST MEN HAVE PASSED TO SUPREME POWER, IT HAS CONTRIBUTED TO EMANCIPATE MANKIND FROM THE THRALDOM OF TRADITION AND TO ELEVATE THEM INTO A LARGER, FREER LIFE, WITH A BROADER OUTLOOK ON THE WORLD. THIS IS NO SMALL SERVICE RENDERED TO HUMANITY. AND WHEN WE REMEMBER FURTHER THAT IN ANOTHER DIRECTION MAGIC HAS PAVED THE WAY FOR SCIENCE, WE ARE FORCED TO ADMIT THAT IF THE BLACK ART HAS DONE MUCH EVIL, IT HAS ALSO BEEN THE SOURCE OF MUCH GOOD; THAT IF IT IS THE CHILD OF ERROR, IT HAS YET BEEN THE MOTHER OF FREEDOM AND TRUTH.

Frazer

1854-1941. Frazer's *Golden Bough* was first published in 1890. He has recently fallen quite out of favour, yet as late as the 1950s it could be written that:

"...psychoanalysis and the [Frazerian]*Cambridge school of anthropology have been complacently embraced by our contemporaries- so much so that it almost looks as if these two persuasions were dividing the entire realm of non scientific speculation between them".*

Psychoanalysis has survived, despite its questionable scientific status. Frazer is contemptuously dismissed, the continued popularity of *The Golden Bough* grudgingly described as that of a 'middlebrow classic'. Much of the hostility to Frazer may be political. To think of ideas in terms of magick is to loosen their hold upon us.

With his ideas like the sacrifice of the god-king Frazer inspired imaginative writers like Margaret Murray and Robert Graves, as well as T S Eliot and Crowley.

Stories of his Magick

The original Mr Watkins of Watkins' famous occult bookshop just off the Charing Cross Road asked him to demonstrate his magick, so Crowley told him to close his eyes for a few seconds. When he opened them all the books had vanished from his shelves.

In response to another request Crowley walks behind a man walking in the street, imitating his gait, then drops down suddenly. The man does the same, to his own complete astonishment.

Dylan Thomas was sitting in a pub when Crowley walked in, bought a drink, and sat some distance away with his back to him. Thomas started doodling nervously. After Crowley finished his drink he left the pub, handing as he passed a piece of paper on which was a copy of everything Thomas had just drawn.

Previous Incarnations

Mysticism

Crowley was interested in all forms of mysticism, including Christian. He regarded himself as more naturally gifted in mysticism than he was in magick.

THE PATH OF THE MYSTICK HATH THIS PITFALL: THAT THOUGH HE UNITE HIMSELF WITH HIS GOD, HIS MODE IS TO WITHDRAW FROM THAT WHICH HIMSEEMETH IS NOT GOD, WHEREWITH HE AFFIRMETH AND CONFIRMETH THE DEMON, THAT IS, DUALITY.

Crowley's *Holy Books* have been hailed as among the very best things he wrote, ranking with *Magick* and *The Confessions*. To some they are the perfection of mystical experience.

"THEY ARE GEMS IN THE DIADEM OF HIS SPIRITUAL ACHIEVEMENT, HAVING NO COUNTERPART WHATEVER IN THE LITERATURE OF MYSTICAL EXPERIENCE". (REGARDIE)

Religion

Out of Thelema he created a new Religion.

One of life affirmation, offering survival after death in whatever form you might desire it.

Accepting Freud's reduction of religion to sex, he found a place for religion nonetheless.

RELIGION IS AN ILLUSION AND IT DERIVES ITS STRENGTH FROM THE FACT THAT IT FALLS IN WITH OUR INSTINCTUAL DESIRES.

WHEN YOU HAVE PROVED THAT GOD IS MERELY A NAME FOR THE SEX INSTINCT, IT APPEARS TO ME NOT FAR TO THE PERCEPTION THAT THE SEX INSTINCT IS GOD.

SPECIAL MESSENGERS OF THE INFINITE WHO INITIATE PERIODS

SIDDARTHA (BUDDHA)

KRISHNA

CHRIST (INCLUDED UNDER DIONYSUS)

TAHUTI (THOTH)

MOSES

LAO-TZU

DIONYSUS

MAHMUD

PERDURABO

Mohammed

"HOW MOHAMMED, WHO FOLLOWETH, IS DARKENED AND CONFUSED BY HIS NEARNESS TO OUR OWN TIME, SO THAT I SAY NOT SAVE WITH DIFFIDENCE THAT HIS WORD **ALLH** MAY MEAN THIS OR THAT..."

بسم الله الرحمن الرحيم
اللهم صل على محمد
وعلى ال محمد كما صليت
على ابراهيم وعلى ال ابراهيم
انك حميد مجيد
اللهم بارك على محمد وعلى
ال محمد كما باركت على
ابراهيم وعلى ال ابراهيم
انك حميد مجيد

Regardie noted Crowley's profound admiration for the so called 'manliness of the Arab, his courage and ferocity'.

"...HIS WILL WAS TO UNITE ALL MEN IN ONE REASONABLE FAITH: TO MAKE POSSIBLE INTERNATIONAL CO-OPERATION IN SCIENCE. YET, BECAUSE HE AROSE IN THE TIME OF THE GREATEST POSSIBLE CORRUPTION AND DARKNESS, WHEN EVERY CIVILISATION AND EVERY RELIGION HAD FALLEN INTO RUIN, BY THE MALICE OF THE GREAT SORCERER OF NAZARETH..."

76

Nietzsche too preferred Islam to Christianity.

Our Lady Babalon

In the Book of Revelation she is the Whore who rideth upon the Beast.

"SO HE CARRIED ME AWAY IN THE SPIRIT INTO THE WILDERNESS: AND I SAW A WOMAN SIT UPON A SCARLET COLOURED BEAST, FULL OF NAMES OF BLASPHEMY, HAVING SEVEN HEADS AND TEN HORNS..."

"...AND THE WOMAN WAS ARRAYED IN PURPLE AND SCARLET COLOUR, AND DECKED WITH GOLD AND PRECIOUS STONES AND PEARLS, HAVING A GOLDEN CUP IN HER HAND FULL OF ABOMINATIONS AND FILTHINESS OF HER FORNICATION... AND UPON HER FOREHEAD WAS A NAME WRITTEN, **MYSTERY, BABYLON THE GREAT, THE MOTHER OF HARLOTS AND ABOMINATIONS OF THE EARTH...**"

"...AND I SAW THE WOMAN DRUNKEN WITH THE BLOOD OF THE SAINTS, AND WITH THE BLOOD OF THE MARTYRS OF JESUS: AND WHEN I SAW HER, I WONDERED WITH GREAT ADMIRATION."

Other influences on Crowley's conception were Baudelaire's poetry and Wagner's idea of corrupt civilisation.

Some of his lovers took on this identity, becoming his Scarlet Women. Leah Hirsig, hymned as Leah Sublime, arguably the greatest of them, lived her role to the full.

Seduction

He was extremely attractive to women. He gave his women animal names...

THE APE

THE DOG

THE CAMEL

as well as spiritual ones, such as:

ALOSTRAEL and SISTER CYPRIS.

A wealthy lady felt a powerful presence behind her as she stood outside the Ritz in Piccadilly. It was Crowley, whom she had never met before. They disappeared into the hotel together and two weeks later her marriage broke up.

A 19 year old girl came up to the Beast on the day of the libel verdict which she called '*the wickedest thing since the crucifixion*' and offered to bear him a child, which she went on to do. She was with him when he died.

The A∴A∴

Crowley eventually left the Golden Dawn amid much conflict and division. He founded his own Magickal order, the A∴A∴ - Argentium Astrum or Silver Star.

THE METHOD OF SCIENCE, THE AIM OF RELIGION.

He published *The Equinox*, a journal of esoteric and thelemic matters which built into an encyclopaedia.

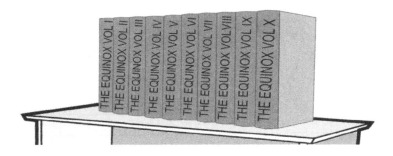

OTO

He was invited to join the secret society of the OTO, which he came to lead and converted to Thelema.

THIS WAS THE *ORDO TEMPLIS ORIENTIS* WHICH STILL EXISTS.

INSPIRED BY THE MEDIAEVAL KNIGHTS TEMPLAR THEY PRACTICED SEX MAGICK.

Knights Templar

When the mediaeval Knights Templar were crushed with the aid of the Inquisition in the 13th century, they were accused of various blasphemous practices, including worshiping an Idol known as Baphomet.

BAPHOMET BECAME ANOTHER OF CROWLEY'S TITLES.

A mystery surrounding the name was cleared up by a spirit that appeared to the Camel, one of his women.

FOR SIX YEARS AND MORE I HAD TRIED TO DISCOVER THE PROPER WAY TO SPELL THIS NAME. ... SO FAR, THE WIZARD HAD SHOWN GREAT QUALITIES! HE HAD CLEARED UP THE ETYMOLOGICAL PROBLEM AND SHOWN WHY THE TEMPLARS SHOULD HAVE GIVEN THE NAME BAPHOMET TO THEIR SO-CALLED IDOL. BAPHOMET WAS FATHER MITHRAS, THE CUBICAL STONE WHICH WAS THE CORNER OF THE TEMPLE.

The Eleventh Degree

Within the symbolism of the OTO this was homosexual magick.
Crowley practiced it with Victor Neuburg.

SWEET WIZARD, IN WHOSE FOOTSTEPS I HAVE TROD
UNTO THE SHRINE OF THE MOST OBSCENE GOD,
SO STEEP THE PATHWAY IS, I MAY NOT KNOW,
UNTIL I REACH THE SUMMIT, WHERE I GO.
MY LOVE IS DEATHLESS AS THE SPRINGS OF TRUTH,
MY LOVE IS PURE AS IS THE DAWN OF YOUTH,
BUT ALL MY BEING THROBS IN RHYTHM WITH THINE,
WHO LEADEST ON TO THE HORIZON LINE.

Neuburg was a young Jewish poet who came to adore Crowley.

Together they explored the magical system of Aethyrs received from spirits by the Elizabethan occultists John Dee and Edward Kelly, in a hitherto unknown language called Enochian.

In the Sahara desert Neuburg and Crowley fought with the terrifying demon Choronzon in what, as Mistlberger observes, was an archetypal Shamanistic initiation.

Later they fell out badly.

True Story

In Algeria he shaved Neuburg's head, leaving just two tufts like devil's horns, and led him around like a pet.

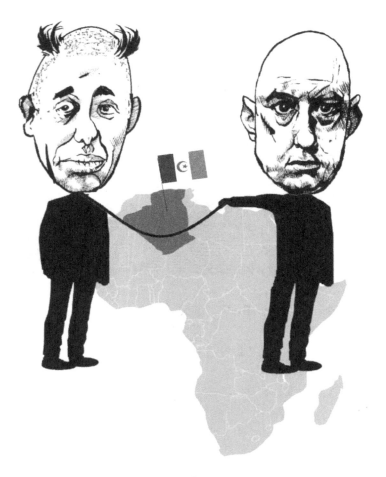

The Abbey at Cefalu

At Cefalu in Sicily where he lived for a while in the 1920s he established a proto-hippy commune. It was inspired by the Abbey in Rabelais' Gargantua and Pantagruel whose motto was...

FAY CE QUE VOUDRA (DO WHAT THOU WILT).

As an experiment in living it ended in failure, death and drug addiction.

"THE PROFESSED AIM OF THE THELEMITE CREED IS TO PENETRATE INTO THE DEEPER MYSTERIES OF CREATION, AND TO FREE THE SPIRIT FROM THE TRAMMELS OF THE FLESH. AS FAR AS I COULD GATHER, THE METHOD OF LIBERATION THEY ADOPT IS TO SATIATE THE SENSES WITH THE IDEA OF, SO TO SPEAK, COMING OUT AT THE OTHER SIDE. IT IS NOT DIFFICULT TO REALISE THAT SOME OF THE WEAKER VESSELS NEVER SUCCEED IN EMERGING, OR PERHAPS DO NOT EVEN WISH TO DO SO". (BETTY MAY- IN HER AUTOBIOGRAPHICAL **TIGER WOMAN**).

Reputation

Was he a mere charlatan or the greatest religious genius of modern times? Israel Regardie wrote that: "everyone must agree that Crowley was illuminated".

What might this mean?

Charisma

Cammell invokes Goethe's idea of daemonic characters to explain his charisma.

> THEY ARE SELDOM DISTINGUISHED BY GOODNESS OF HEART: A TREMENDOUS ENERGY SEEMS TO EMANATE FROM THEM AND THEY EXERCISE A WONDERFUL POWER OVER ALL CREATURES... SELDOM IF EVER DO THEY FIND THEIR EQUALS AMONG THEIR CONTEMPORARIES, NOTHING CAN VANQUISH THEM BUT THE UNIVERSE ITSELF WITH WHICH THEY HAVE BEGUN THE FRAY.

He compared Crowley to Hitler, Napoleon, Rasputin, Genghis Khan and Tamberlaine.

What was the relation between his personal charisma and the value of his ideas? How does his charisma relate to his notoriety and his Antichrist role?

Role Model

He had an enviable level of charisma that was often described as hypnotic power. In his lifetime he inspired great admiration in some very intelligent men. Since his death he has offered a role model for many others.

He had his own role models, notably Sir Richard Burton and S L 'Macgregor' Mathers, though he fell out with the latter.

Mrs Grundy

Mrs Grundy, personification of the tyranny of conventional propriety, is also known anagrammatically as the goddess Ydgrun (Samuel Butler).

Given that a large part of Crowley's creative achievement was concerned with defying and provoking Mrs Grundy, it is hardly surprising that she should have hit back.

Crowley was hated and reviled.

HIS WORK, CONSIDERED AS WHOLE, IS A BLEND OF BLASPHEMY, FILTH AND NONSENSE. THE NONSENSE IS FLAVOURED WITH MYSTICISM... MOST OF THE POEMS ARE PORNOGRAPHIC, MANY OF THEM REVOLTING, AND ALL THEM THE PRODUCT OF DISEASED MIND AND A DEBASED CHARACTER... THROUGH ALL HIS WORK RUNS A LOATHING OF CHRISTIANITY.

Depravity

Was his whole persona just a formula for seducing women? Devil or god? Attacked by the press, he was called...

Megalomaniac or Master?

A key question is how much his character flaws are just weaknesses and vices, or whether they express some esoteric meaning.

I DO NOT WISH TO ARGUE THAT THE DOCTRINES OF JESUS, THEY AND THEY ALONE, HAVE DEGRADED THE WORLD TO ITS PRESENT CONDITION. I TAKE IT THAT CHRISTIANITY IS NOT ONLY THE CAUSE BUT THE SYMPTOM OF **SLAVERY**.

Was his living out the Beast role just self indulgence or paradoxically a sign of unselfish dedication to the good of humanity? Was he doing good by liberating mankind from the curse of the slave gods?

Unlikely Stories

Hitler's associate Ludendorff got the swastika symbol from Crowley, who later gave Churchill the V sign as a lunar counter to the solar magic of the swastika.

He practised human sacrifice. This one comes from taking literally the chapter *On the Bloody Sacrifice* in *Magick in Theory and Practice*:

"FOR THE HIGHEST SPIRITUAL WORKING ONE MUST ACCORDINGLY CHOOSE THAT VICTIM WHICH CONTAINS THE GREATEST AND PUREST FORCE. A MALE CHILD OF PERFECT INNOCENCE AND HIGH INTELLIGENCE IS THE MOST SATISFACTORY AND SUITABLE VICTIM. IT APPEARS FROM THE MAGICAL RECORDS OF FRATER PERDURABO THAT HE MADE THIS PARTICULAR SACRIFICE ON AN AVERAGE ABOUT 150 TIMES A YEAR BETWEEN 1912 AND 1928."

This should properly be read as a joke.

George W Bush is Crowley's grandson.

Ragged Ragtime Girls

In 1913 he travelled to Moscow with a troupe of chorus girls called the Ragged Ragtime Girls who had played a season in London. Leila Waddell played the violin.

Moscow was a city that entranced Crowley.

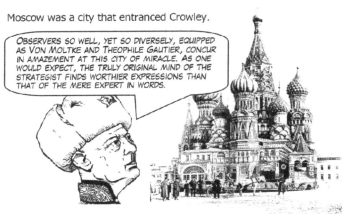

OBSERVERS SO WELL, YET SO DIVERSELY, EQUIPPED AS VON MOLTKE AND THEOPHILE GAUTIER, CONCUR IN AMAZEMENT AT THIS CITY OF MIRACLE. AS ONE WOULD EXPECT, THE TRULY ORIGINAL MIND OF THE STRATEGIST FINDS WORTHIER EXPRESSIONS THAN THAT OF THE MERE EXPERT IN WORDS.

Criticism

A common criticism of Crowley was that he was not a nice person, and that everyone associated with him came a cropper. That one would have had no interest in becoming one of his followers.

He treated his scarlet women badly.

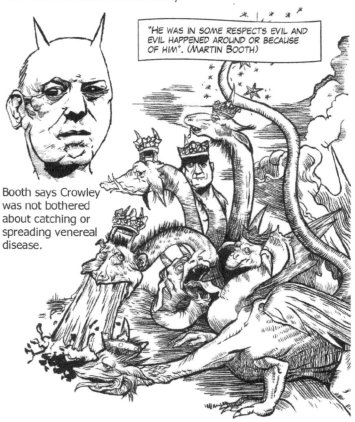

"HE WAS IN SOME RESPECTS EVIL AND EVIL HAPPENED AROUND OR BECAUSE OF HIM". (MARTIN BOOTH)

Booth says Crowley was not bothered about catching or spreading venereal disease.

Mistreatment of Women

He allowed Scarlet Woman Leah to starve after she went off with his disciple Norman Mudd. He joked callously when his second wife was admitted to a lunatic asylum. Having written passionate love poetry (Rosa Mundi) about his first wife he wrote very unpleasantly about her in the later poem Rosa Decidua.

I AM DUMB WITH RAPTURE OF THY LOVELINESS.
ALL METRES MATCH AND MINGLE; ALL WORDS TIRE;
ALL LIGHTS, ALL SOUNDS, ALL PERFUMES, ALL GOLD STRESS
OF THE HONEY-PALATE, ALL SOFT STROKES EXPIRE
IN ABJECT AGONY OF BROKEN SENSE
TO HYMN THE EMOTION TENSE
OF SOMEWHAT HIGHER -- O! HOW HIGHEST! -- THAN ALL
THEIR MYSTERY: FALL, O FALL,
YE UNAVAILING EAGLE-FLIGHTS OF SONG!
O WIFE! THESE DO THEE WRONG.

MINUTE INVADING WRINKLES WHERE THE FLESH
IS SOAKED AWAY BY THE FOUL THING WITHIN
HER SOUL; THE BLOOM SO FAINT AND FRESH
SMUDGED TO A SMOKY GLOW AS ONE MAY SEE
AT SUNSET IN THE FACTORY LANDS; THE LIPS
THINNED AND THEIR COLOUR SICKENED INTO SLATE;
THE EYES LIKE COMMON GLASS; THE HAIR'S GLOSS DULL;
THE MUSCLES GONE, ALL PENDULOUS WITH FAT...

In his defence, Regardie, with his background in psychoanalysis, says all people have ambivalence towards their lovers and that Crowley was just more honest about it.

In recent years he has faced accusations of...

Racism and Sexism

On the basis of some of his statements.

Thelemites defend him on the ground that...

THERE IS NO LAW BEYOND DO WHAT THOU WILT

...and that accordingly it would be wrong to constrain him under some alternative moral rule. Like a Zen or Sufi master he aims to enlighten us by shocking us out of our habitual thought patterns.

Women

"A MAN'S ADULTERIES ARE TOKENS OF HIGH SPIRIT, A WOMAN'S BETRAYAL OF OUR TRUST IN HER, STUPIDITY AND COWARDICE. WE DESPISE THE DRUDGE HUSBAND WHOM WE CUCKOLD, KICK THE FAT RUMP OF THE DULL DUPE BONACIEUX. WE DESPISE ALSO THE COW-MOTHER TYPE OF FEMALE, BUT WE RESPECT SEMIRAMIS, CLEOPATRA, CATHERINE OF RUSSIA, OR, FOR OTHER TYPES OF EXPLOITS, SAPPHO, LADY MACBETH. OR JOAN OF ARC..."

"...IT IS ONLY OUR WISH TO KILL COMPETITION THAT MAKES US PRETEND WE WANT TO BE RESPECTABLE, AND WOMEN VIRTUOUS, HUMANITY (IN SHORT) TO PLAY THE FEMALE WHILE WE DO OUR MALE WILL."

So unlike the Christian God who:

"...ONLY DREW THE MORAL LINE AT ANY SELF ASSERTION THE PART OF WOMAN... IN ANY ABBEY OF THELEMA ANY WOMAN IS WELCOME; THERE SHE IS FREE TO DO HER WILL AND HELD IN HONOUR".

99

Animal Cruelty

Regardie criticised him for enjoying big game hunting.

Once for an important ritual he apparently
crucified a toad, naming it Jesus of Nazareth
and arresting it with the words:

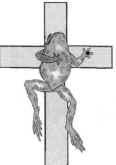

> ALL MY LIFE LONG THOU HAST PLAGUED ME
> AND AFFRONTED ME. IN THY NAME - WITH
> ALL OTHER FREE SOULS IN CHRISTENDOM -
> I HAVE BEEN TORTURED IN MY BOYHOOD; ALL
> DELIGHTS HAVE BEEN FORBIDDEN UNTO ME;
> ALL THAT I HAD HAS BEEN TAKEN FROM ME,
> AND THAT WHICH IS OWED TO ME THEY PAY
> NOT - IN THY NAME. NOW, AT LAST, I HAVE
> THEE; THE SLAVE-GOD IS IN THE POWER OF
> THE LORD OF FREEDOM.

He sacrificed a cat in the Abbey, giving the participants its blood to drink.

To many people these stories are very shocking. That may be the point, as it was in surrealism. Dali claimed to enjoy torturing cats.

Legacy

Crowley was an influence upon the counterculture of the 1960s. He was honoured and admired as a precursor by many hippies.

LOVE IS THE LAW, LOVE UNDER WILL.

Israel Regardie writes with qualified enthusiasm of the psychedelic revolution as a realisation of some of Crowley's ideas. Crowley was admired by Timothy Leary, the high priest of LSD.

TURN ON, TUNE IN, DROP OUT.

I'VE BEEN AN ADMIRER OF ALEISTER CROWLEY. I THINK THAT I'M CARRYING ON MUCH OF THE WORK THAT HE STARTED OVER A HUNDRED YEARS AGO.

"MORE CLOSELY THAN ANYBODY ELSE, HE (LEARY) SEEMS TO HAVE APPROACHED THE ATTITUDES OF ALEISTER CROWLEY ALMOST EXACTLY." (ISRAEL REGARDIE)

Other sixties gurus have been linked to Crowley. (Anti-) psychiatrist RD Laing was attacked in the following terms:

"IT IS IN MILIEUS WHICH INVOKE VISITATION BY INDISCRIMINATE ECSTASY THAT LAING'S WRITINGS HAVE THEIR PROVENANCE, AND IT IS IN A PERIOD CHARACTERIZED BY ALEISTER CROWLEY REDIVIVUS THAT THEY RESONATE." (DAVID MARTIN 'TRACTS AGAINST THE TIMES' P.69)

INSANITY - A PERFECTLY RATIONAL ADJUSTMENT TO AN INSANE WORLD.

It might be objected that Crowley's ecstasies were not exactly indiscriminate and the contempt which people often felt for him discounted the powerful intellect informing his creative achievement.

Punk

The Punk that succeeded the hippy movement in the 1970s found other aspects to admire in Crowley. Peace and love had given way to a new aggression.

Art

Many of his pranks might be appreciated in a modern context if thought of as Concept or Performance Art.

He gave public performances of the rites of Eleusis at Caxton Hall London, with his current scarlet woman, Leila Waddell, playing the violin.

He allegedly fed the audience with hallucinogenic drugs.

Sex

When Crowley says that not one person in ten thousand achieve sexual balance that implies that all conventional sexual wisdom is wrong. Saying that is easier than saying what is right.

THERE IS NOTHING UNCLEAN OR DEGRADING IN ANY MANIFESTATION WHATEVER OF THE SEXUAL INSTINCT, BECAUSE, WITHOUT EXCEPTION, EVERY ACT IS AN IMPULSIVELY PROJECTED IMAGE OF THE WILL OF THE INDIVIDUAL WHO, WHETHER MAN OR WOMAN, IS A STAR; THE PENNSYLVANIAN WITH HIS PIG NO LESS THAN THE SPIRIT WITH MARY.

It would be an understatement to say his own sex life was rich and varied.

Pervert

For the public of his day he was a vile pervert. He practised coprophagy and sadomasochism.

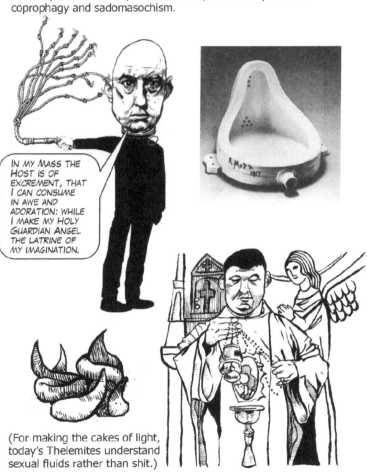

(For making the cakes of light, today's Thelemites understand sexual fluids rather than shit.)

Kinks

At the Abbey there was bisexuality and ritual bestiality. There was no serious suspicion of incest or paedophilia (in contrast with his near contemporary Eric Gill, the Catholic artist, at his own commune).

However he was crassly accused of sacrificing children.

BLOOD SWEAT AND CUM AND THE SLIME FROM HER BUMB.

He glorified bodily excrescences. For Crowley every sex act had a religious significance.

Drugs

He was introduced to drug experimentation by Allan Bennett.

TO WORSHIP ME TAKE WINE AND STRANGE DRUGS WHEREOF I WILL TELL MY PROPHET... THEY SHALL NOT HARM YE AT ALL.

Mrs Grundy did not like this either.

Drug Culture

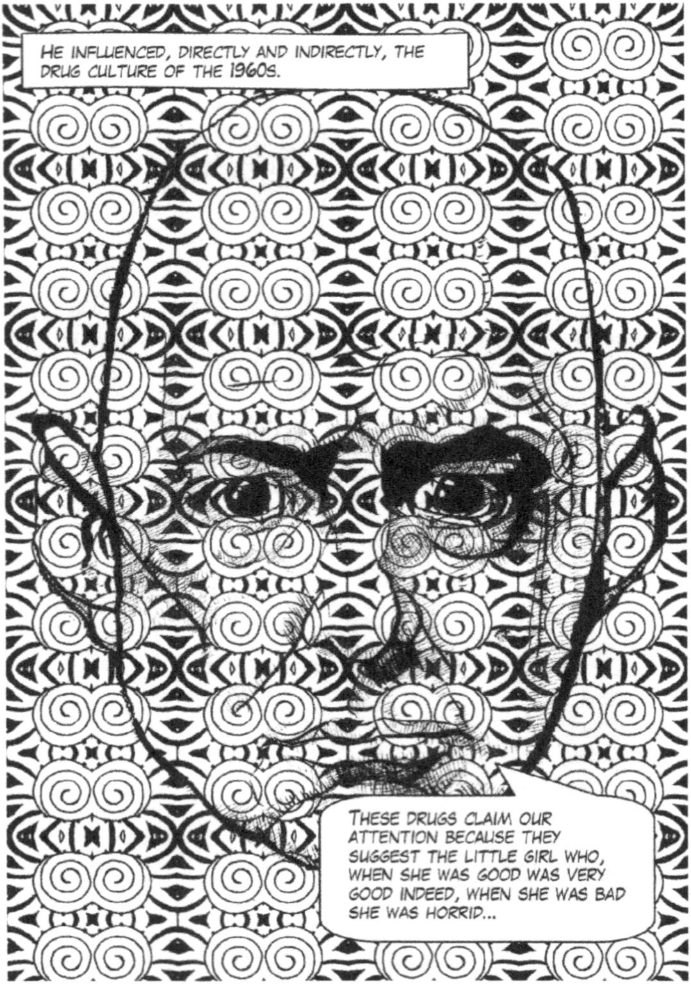
HE INFLUENCED, DIRECTLY AND INDIRECTLY, THE DRUG CULTURE OF THE 1960S.
THESE DRUGS CLAIM OUR ATTENTION BECAUSE THEY SUGGEST THE LITTLE GIRL WHO, WHEN SHE WAS GOOD WAS VERY GOOD INDEED, WHEN SHE WAS BAD SHE WAS HORRID...

He wrote an essay on the psychology of hashish in terms of the Abidhamma philosophy of Theravada Buddhism. Regardie suggests the essay is more relevant to the experience of LSD.
Mystic trances based upon the Buddhist Skhandas (elements of experience):

HERE, GENTLEMEN, ARE A NUMBER OF GENUINE MYSTIC STATES... IN MY VIEW MOST OF THE GREAT MEN OF THE WORLD HAVE KNOWN THEM... BUT AT THE VERY LEAST THESE STATES ARE OF THE MOST EXTRAORDINARY INTEREST. EVEN AS INSANITIES THEY WOULD DEMAND THE STRICTEST INVESTIGATION FROM THE LIGHT THEY THROW ON THE WORKINGS OF THE BRAIN.

VINNANAM

SANKHARA

SANNA

VEDANA

NAMA RUPA

"...FORTUNATELY WE HAVE, IN THE BUDDHIST SKANDHAS AND THE THREE CHARACTERISTICS WHICH DENY THEM, A SCHEME EASILY ASSIMILABLE TO WESTERN PSYCHOLOGY."

He experimented with ether, mescaline, and many other drugs. He wrote an essay on cocaine. He developed problems of addiction to both heroin and cocaine.

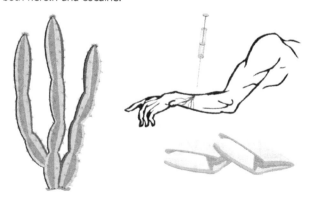

Rock 'n' Roll

Rock stars who admired or mentioned
him include John Lennon, Jim Morrison,
Jimmy Page, David Bowie, Ozzy Osborne
and the Rolling Stones.

THE WHOLE BEATLE IDEA WAS TO
DO WHAT YOU WANT, RIGHT? TO
TAKE YOUR OWN RESPONSIBILITY, DO
WHAT YOU WANT AND TRY NOT TO
HARM OTHER PEOPLE, RIGHT? DO
WHAT THOU WILST, AS LONG AS
IT DOESN'T HURT SOMEBODY...

Much in Crowley was congenial to the rebellious and hedonistic
attitudes of rock music.

Downfall

He tried to make money by suing for libel. Some of his poetry was read out in court.

Crowley lost the case. He was bankrupted. But famous.

Charlatan or Mystic Genius?

In assuming the grade of Ipsissimus he effectively anointed himself God.

He indulged gratifying fantasies of grandeur, with much self praise.

> MY CERTAINTY THAT DESTINY IS "GOOD"...

> ...RESTS ON ITS PICKING ME FOR BUDDHAHOOD.

Some take his claims at face value.

If we don't want to take his claims about himself at face value we may seek his message in the fact he felt able to make them.

Esoteric wisdom is a matter of reading between the lines.

> IN PLATO'S *THEAGES* IT IS WRITTEN: 'EACH ONE OF US WOULD LIKE TO BE MASTER OVER ALL MEN, IF POSSIBLE, AND BEST OF ALL GOD.' THIS ATTITUDE MUST EXIST AGAIN.

A New Order?

For the Tantrics, the breaking of taboos had value in itself. Crowley's attitude was similar.

"ALL MORAL CODES ARE WORTHLESS IN THEMSELVES; YET IN EVERY NEW CODE THERE IS HOPE."

Conformism was generally to be avoided.

"THE DEAD DOG FLOATS WITH THE STREAM."

Surrealism

There is some parallel with the surrealists. Younger than Crowley, they too were inspired by Nietzsche, sought visionary experiences and were concerned to épater le bourgeois.

ANDRE BRETON, AUTHOR OF THE SURREALIST MANIFESTO.

EVERYTHING TENDS TO MAKE US BELIEVE THAT THERE EXISTS A CERTAIN POINT OF THE MIND AT WHICH LIFE AND DEATH, THE REAL AND THE IMAGINED, PAST AND FUTURE, THE COMMUNICABLE AND THE INCOMMUNICABLE, HIGH AND LOW, CEASE TO BE PERCEIVED AS CONTRADICTIONS.

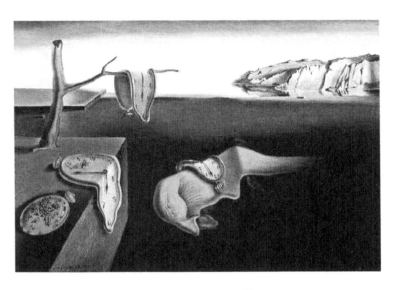

SURREALISM IS DESTRUCTIVE, BUT IT DESTROYS ONLY WHAT IT CONSIDERS TO BE SHACKLES LIMITING OUR VISION.

Modernism

The great impresario of literary modernism, Ezra Pound, insisted upon Crowley's exclusion from the modern movement. As a romantic decadent, Crowley represented everything Pound was trying to get away from. Also the popular impact of his persona clashed with the elitism of the modern movement. It was considered a sell-out.

Pound's attitude was not shared by all critics, but prevailed.
A R Orage, promoter of modern literary and intellectual movements, editor of the influential journal *The New Age* wanted to include Crowley.

His girlfriend Beatrice Hastings (who later modelled for Modigliani) put a stop to it:

> I FOUND A COLLECTION OF WORKS ON SORCERY. UP TO THIS TIME ORAGE'S FRIEND WAS NOT MR HOLBROOK JACKSON, WHO THOUGHT HE WAS, BUT MR ALEISTER CROWLEY. WELL I CONSIGNED ALL THE BOOKS AND EQUINOXES AND SORCERY DESIGNS TO THE DUSTBIN.

But with the break-up of modernism came:

Pop

His showmanship was no longer a disqualification, nor was his popular appeal.

ONCE YOU 'GOT' POP, YOU COULD NEVER SEE A SIGN AGAIN THE SAME WAY AGAIN. AND ONCE YOU THOUGHT POP, YOU COULD NEVER SEE AMERICA THE SAME WAY AGAIN.

DON'T PAY ANY ATTENTION TO WHAT THEY WRITE ABOUT YOU. JUST MEASURE IT IN INCHES.

...and many of the modernist objections fade away.

Science

Crowley liked to keep up to date with the science of his day and some of his recommended reading, like the speculations of CR Hinton on the fourth dimension is an illuminating background to any of the popular books on relativity that are much read these days.

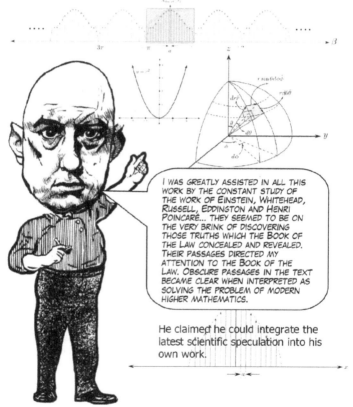

I WAS GREATLY ASSISTED IN ALL THIS WORK BY THE CONSTANT STUDY OF THE WORK OF EINSTEIN, WHITEHEAD, RUSSELL, EDDINGTON AND HENRI POINCARÉ... THEY SEEMED TO BE ON THE VERY BRINK OF DISCOVERING THOSE TRUTHS WHICH THE BOOK OF THE LAW CONCEALED AND REVEALED. THEIR PASSAGES DIRECTED MY ATTENTION TO THE BOOK OF THE LAW. OBSCURE PASSAGES IN THE TEXT BECAME CLEAR WHEN INTERPRETED AS SOLVING THE PROBLEM OF MODERN HIGHER MATHEMATICS.

He claimed he could integrate the latest scientific speculation into his own work.

Leg Pulls

Not everything Crowley says is to be taken literally. He constantly plays jokes on his readers. How much this interferes with what he really wants to communicate is questionable. He is passionate to get his message across, but would presumably want to be read between the lines.

NATURE IS FALSE, BUT I'M A BIT OF A LIAR MYSELF.

As Scottish architect William Stirling wrote in *The Canon - An Exposition of the Pagan Mystery Perpetuated in the Cabala as the Rule of all the Arts* (1897), one of the books of Crowley's reading list:

> "RHETORIC IS THE SCIENCE AND ART OF SAYING ONE THING WHILE MEANING ANOTHER."

Postmodernism

Foucault's exposure of the limitations of post enlightenment scientific logicality and appreciation of exotic traditions had long been commonplace among Thelemites.

Crowley, however was more of a romantic than a postmodernist. There is much in him with which postmodernists should not be happy. The postmodernists had a different project, empowering certain excluded groups.

Nevertheless, the pomos have appropriated Nietzsche so why not Crowley?

Ego

Postmodernist ideas about non existence of ego find a lot of resonance in Crowley. Writing of himself:

"...HE HAD INDEED GOT RID OF HIS SENSE OF PERSONAL SELF."

And of the Buddha:

"...AND HIS WORD WAS ANATTA, FOR THE ROOT OF HIS WHOLE DOCTRINE WAS THAT THERE IS NO ATMAN OR SOUL AS MEN ILL TRANSLATE IT, MEANING A SUBSTANCE INCAPABLE OF CHANGE."

NO FIXED SELF.

NO PRESENCE-TO-SELF, OR SELF-CONTAINED IDENTITY.

Paradox

How could such a massive ego square with the egolessness demanded by the mystic and on which Crowley so often insisted?

For Bennett, as a Buddhist, individualism not only contradicted Anatta but was a curse:

TILL IN OUR OWN TIMES A NIETZSCHE CAN FIND MANIFOLD DISCIPLES FOR HIS DOCTRINE OF SELFHOOD APOTHEOSISED:-'THE GREAT BLONDE BEAST' UPHELD AS AN IDEAL TO BE FOLLOWED...

Crowley disagreed.

KEEP THE PLANES SEPARATE.

He would say that there is no clash.

THE LAW OF THELEMA AVOWS AND JUSTIFIES SELFISHNESS; IT CONFIRMS THE INMOST CONVICTION OF EACH ONE OF US THAT HE IS THE CENTRE OF THE COSMOS.

But then he had come to reject Buddhism.

Political Thelema

In the 1930s he proposed Thelema as a political philosophy, an alternative to communism, fascism and democracy.

He wrote to Walter Duranty about the prospects for his ideas in Stalin's Russia (naturally the reply was discouraging).

His German Disciple Martha Kuntzel tried to convert Hitler to Thelema, sending him a copy of *The Book of the Law*.

Crowley supported the republican side in the Spanish Civil War.

Appreciation

How to appreciate him? Even many who disapproved were deeply fascinated.

> EXPLAIN ME THE RIDDLE OF THIS MAN! (CAMMELL)

To do this we need to negotiate the strange framework of his thought. He did not want to overthrow rationalism. He would leave the perspective of sceptical materialism intact, only reserving the right to experience others.

Dualism Perverted?

"AT THE ROOT OF ALL SATANIC SYSTEMS YOU WILL FIND 'THE WORSHIP OF THE BAD PRINCIPLE PLACED UPON A FOOTING OF PERFECT EQUALITY WITH THE GOOD'. IN CROWLEY'S OPINION THE MORE EXPERIENCES AN INDIVIDUAL COULD CROWD INTO LIFE, ALIKE THE BEST AND THE WORST, THE MOST LAUDABLE AND THE MOST REPREHENSIBLE, THE GREATER WAS HIS FULFILMENT AND THE FURTHER HE ADVANCED TOWARDS ULTIMATE ATTAINMENT..."

"...IN THIS MARCH AND COUNTER MARCH OF EXPERIENCE, THE WILL- THE TRUE WILL- OF THE INDIVIDUAL WAS TO BE THE SOLE COMMANDING OFFICER, THE SOLE GUIDE AND ARBITER. THIS VIEW OF LIFE, AND OF WHAT WAS MAN'S OBJECTIVE IN LIFE (DERIVED LARGELY FROM BURTON'S KASIDAH) DOMINATE CROWLEY'S PHILOSOPHY." (CAMMELL)

One response to the threat presented by his ideas is to deny all meaning to them.

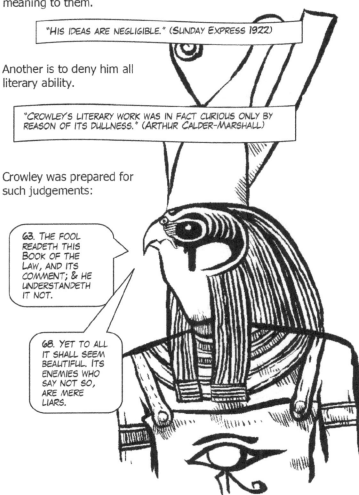

"HIS IDEAS ARE NEGLIGIBLE." (SUNDAY EXPRESS 1922)

Another is to deny him all literary ability.

"CROWLEY'S LITERARY WORK WAS IN FACT CURIOUS ONLY BY REASON OF ITS DULLNESS." (ARTHUR CALDER-MARSHALL)

Crowley was prepared for such judgements:

63. THE FOOL READETH THIS BOOK OF THE LAW, AND ITS COMMENT; & HE UNDERSTANDETH IT NOT.

68. YET TO ALL IT SHALL SEEM BEAUTIFUL. ITS ENEMIES WHO SAY NOT SO, ARE MERE LIARS.

Cool

Though in some respects Crowley may seem well attuned to the zeitgeist, intellectually, for all his depth and brilliance, he is not considered cool.

...LACANIAN ANALYSIS, GYNOCRITICISM, POST-COLONIAL STUDIES.

Very different doctrines have seized the fashionable high ground and currently dominate.

The Esoteric Tradition

Many would say it is right that this should never be part of the mainstream, but aspire to a hidden (occult) influence upon the exoteric.

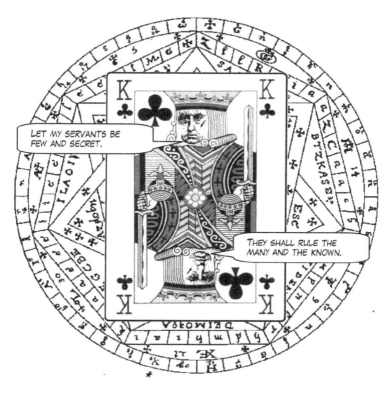

Reading between the lines. Has his influence on the modern world been esoteric?

Academia

In his own day Crowley's ideas attracted highly intelligent young students from Oxford and Cambridge, to the occasional scandal of the college authorities. Recently Crowley has not received much academic attention. One exception is the book *Aleister Crowley and the 20th Century Synthesis of Magick* by David Evans, who as well as a professional academic researcher describes himself as a practising magician.

He feels a need to tell us that Crowley was not a fascist, as if we might be tempted to think he was.

THERE HAS REPORTEDLY BEEN SOME SERIOUS ACADEMIC INTEREST IN THE CZECH REPUBLIC.

Fundies

Some Fundamentalist Christian groups in America regard him as the intellectual force behind what they see as the worst aspects of modern decadence and immorality. This is like taking him at his own estimation as Antichrist.

Presumably he would have been flattered, but would not have considered his work to have been so easily accomplished.

Gnostic Mass

The ritual of the Gnostic mass is a Thelemic religious rite composed by Crowley that is still celebrated in various countries throughout the world, often with a naked priestess.

THE HIGH ALTAR... SHOULD BE COVERED WITH A CRIMSON ALTAR CLOTH ON WHICH MAY BE EMBROIDERED FLEUR-DE-LYS IN GOLD, OR A SUNBLAZE, OR OTHER SUITABLE EMBLEM.

The Gnostic Saints

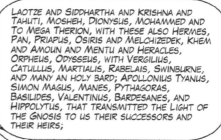

LAOTZE AND SIDDHARTHA AND KRISHNA AND TAHUTI, MOSHEH, DIONYSUS, MOHAMMED AND TO MEGA THERION, WITH THESE ALSO HERMES, PAN, PRIAPUS, OSIRIS AND MELCHIZEDEK, KHEM AND AMOUN AND MENTU AND HERACLES, ORPHEUS, ODYSSEUS, WITH VERGILIUS, CATULLUS, MARTIALIS, RABELAIS, SWINBURNE, AND MANY AN HOLY BARD; APOLLONIUS TYANUS, SIMON MAGUS, MANES, PYTHAGORAS, BASILIDES, VALENTINUS, BARDESANES, AND HIPPOLYTUS, THAT TRANSMITTED THE LIGHT OF THE GNOSIS TO US THEIR SUCCESSORS AND THEIR HEIRS;

... WITH MERLIN, ARTHUR, KAMURET, PARZIVAL, AND MANY ANOTHER, PROPHET, PRIEST AND KING, THAT BORE THE LANCE AND CUP, THE SWORD AND DISK, AGAINST THE HEATHEN; AND THESE ALSO, CAROLUS MAGNUS AND HIS PALADINS, WITH WILLIAM OF SCHYREN, FREDERICK OF HOHENSTAUFEN, ROGER BACON, JACOBUS BURGUNDUS MOLENSIS THE MARTYR, CHRISTIAN ROSENCREUTZ, ULRICH VON HUTTEN, PARACELSUS, MICHAEL MAIER, RODERIC BORGIA POPE ALEXANDER THE SIXTH, JACOB BOEHME, FRANCIS BACON, LORD VERULAM...

... ANDREA, ROBERTUS DE FLUCTIBUS, GIORDANO BRUNO, JOHANNES DEE, SIR EDWARD KELLY, THOMAS VAUGHAN, ELIAS ASHMOLE, MOLINOS, ADAM WEISHAUPT, WOLFGANG VON GOETHE, WILLIAM BLAKE, LUDOVICUS REX BAVARIAE, RICHARD WAGNER, ALPHONSE LOUIS CONSTANT, FRIEDRICH NIETZSCHE, HARGRAVE JENNINGS, FORLONG DUX, SIR RICHARD PAYNE KNIGHT, PAUL GAUGUIN, SIR RICHARD FRANCIS BURTON, DOCTOR GERARD ENCAUSSE, CARL KELLNER, DOCTOR THEODOR REUSS, SIR ALEISTER CROWLEY, KARL JOHANNES GERMER, AND MAJOR GRADY LOUIS MCMURTRY.

Perusing the list of the Gnostic saints we can get a good idea of the tradition that Crowley desired to perpetuate, as well as people he admired.

Occult Tradition

He has contributed considerably to this, and largely dominates it in English speaking countries. The occult tradition has offered a framework on which to hang original ideas. Crowley is read, if only by a select few. His writings and ideas have provided inspiration for the rather different speculations of Chaos Magic and the Typhonian Order of Kenneth Grant.

He has also had a strong influence on the new (or very old) religion of Gardnerian Witchcraft as well as a number of other movements including Scientology and New Age Paganism.

Science Fiction

Unlike his character, which has had a strong presence in many novels from Somerset Maugham's *The Magician* to Anthony Powell's *Dance to the Music of Time*, Crowley's ideas have not had a marked influence on English literature. An exception is the subgenre of science fiction.

Science fiction writers like Robert Heinlein and Richard Anton Wilson have incorporated Crowleyan themes in their books.

Parsons

In his later years Old Crow, as he came to be known, kept an eye on the events across the Atlantic in California, where Jack Parsons, a genius rocket scientist and one of the originators of the American space programme was in charge of the Agape Lodge, a branch of the OTO, living in a thelemic commune in Pasadena.

This was an important source of income for Crowley. Also, he could observe the wild use a younger generation were making of his principles. Crowley struck a note of restraint and caution.

Parsons was relieved of his fortune by science fiction writer L Ron Hubbard, who later went on to found Scientology. In 1952 Parsons blew himself up.

Thought

It is difficult to do justice to the richness of his thought, often expressed with great elegance and literary skill.

WHITE IS WHITE IS THE LASH OF THE OVERSEER, WHITE IS BLACK IS THE WATCHWORD OF THE SLAVE. THE MASTER TAKES NO HEED.

FOR PURE WILL, UNASSUAGED OF PURPOSE, DELIVERED FROM THE LUST OF RESULT, IS EVERY WAY PERFECT.

THE GAME GOES ON, IT MAY HAVE BEEN TOO ROUGH FOR BUDDHA, BUT IT'S, IF ANYTHING, TOO DULL FOR ME!

Alternative

Crowley may be seen as the leading modern representative of a perennial tradition, the permanently subversive alternative. He was sufficiently alternative to be loathed, dismissed and denounced as unclean. This was in the name of the orthodoxy of the day, the supremely confident, not altogether stupid, Christian doctrine, whether or not we call it bigotry, which he openly ridiculed. If we admire him we are ourselves condemned as sick and hateful by that standard.

Many secular minded people also abhorred him, threatening as he did to spoil their visions and plans for humanity. On the positive side, hostility and conflict were a powerful creative stimulus for him, like an alchemical tension generating thought.

Human Relations

Towards those he regarded as his followers he might appear domineering, and worse.

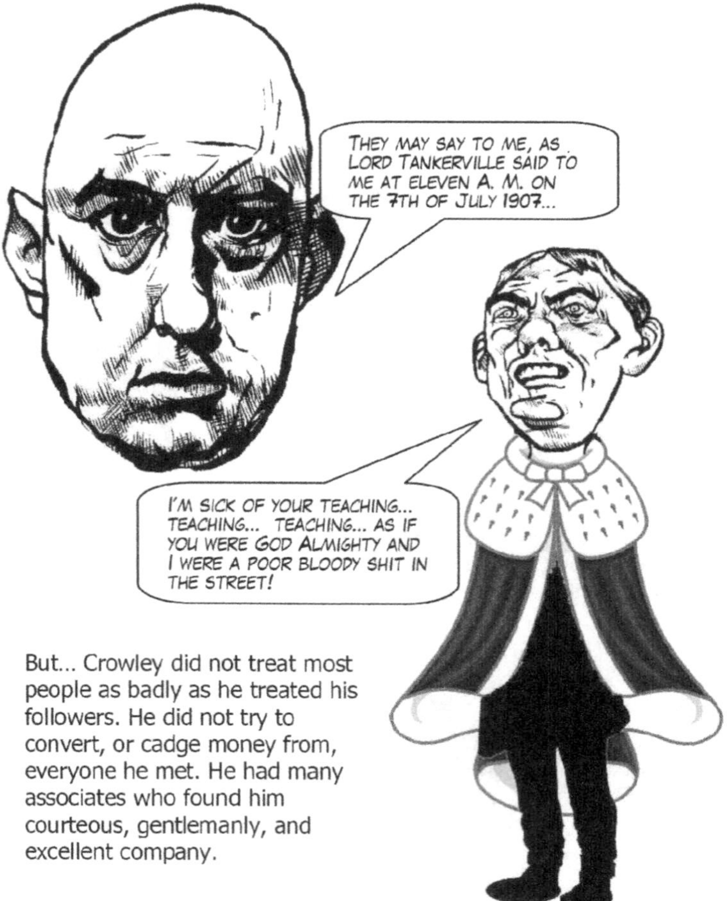
THEY MAY SAY TO ME, AS LORD TANKERVILLE SAID TO ME AT ELEVEN A. M. ON THE 7TH OF JULY 1907...
I'M SICK OF YOUR TEACHING... TEACHING... TEACHING... AS IF YOU WERE GOD ALMIGHTY AND I WERE A POOR BLOODY SHIT IN THE STREET!

But... Crowley did not treat most people as badly as he treated his followers. He did not try to convert, or cadge money from, everyone he met. He had many associates who found him courteous, gentlemanly, and excellent company.

Religious Truth

Crowley published many of his books under the imprint of *The Society for the Propagation of Religious Truth*.

He would explain how much our experience depends upon the concepts within our minds, and how stuck most people are in the presuppositions of their own time. We can aspire to experience different frameworks as something more than entertaining hypotheses. Distinct from its philosophical underpinnings is the idea of religious truth.

Insofar as our philosophy is not invariably defensive, it may seemingly be able to create truth, even God.

Thus Magick proves superior to religion.

Religious truth was something he felt able to communicate through the force of his personal charisma. He has been compared to Rasputin.

Self Praise

As well as a Buddha...

...he was "The New Christ".

...LIKE THE OLD, A FRIEND OF PUBLICANS AND SINNERS.

The surrealist Salvador Dali had just as big an ego. His assertions of his own great genius are also amusing, rebellious and somehow life enhancing.

OH, SALVADOR, NOW YOU KNOW THE TRUTH; IF YOU ACT THE GENIUS YOU WILL BE ONE.

...IT IS NOT NECESSARY FOR THE PUBLIC TO KNOW WHETHER I AM JOKING OR WHETHER I AM SERIOUS, JUST AS IT IS NOT NECESSARY FOR ME TO KNOW IT MYSELF.

Dali, too, was subject to much hostility and contempt which has only recently been muted.

Nietzsche's ego was also huge:

Death

Crowley died in 1947 in Hastings. He was cremated in Brighton and to the scandal of the authorities his friends took over the chapel and performed 'the last ritual' of readings from his own works including the *Hymn to Pan*.

THE GREAT BEASTS COME, IO PAN! I AM BORNE
TO DEATH ON THE HORN
OF THE UNICORN.
I AM PAN! IO PAN! IO PAN PAN! PAN! {VI}
I AM THY MATE, I AM THY MAN,
GOAT OF THY FLOCK, I AM GOLD, I AM GOD,
FLESH TO THY BONE, FLOWER TO THY ROD.

DEATH DOES NOT END LIFE,
IT IS A TEMPORARY PHASE
OF LIFE AS NIGHT AND WINTER
ARE OF TERRESTRIAL ACTIVITY

WITH HOOFS OF STEEL I RACE ON THE ROCKS
THROUGH SOLSTICE STUBBORN TO EQUINOX.
AND I RAVE; AND I RAPE AND I RIP AND I REND
EVERLASTING, WORLD WITHOUT END,
MANNIKIN, MAIDEN, MAENAD, MAN,
IN THE MIGHT OF PAN.

IO PAN! IO PAN PAN! PAN! IO PAN!

How Serious?

How seriously can we take him? He was a tremendous joker, a prankster as well as a great wit. Reading his life and work makes us laugh. That can cheer us up and is arguably a form of enlightenment. He has left us his literary legacy. He impresses by the richness and variety of his writing.

In his own day his presence and significance were greater than most historians allow. *The Freethinker*, a literary magazine in the 1930s was prepared to accept Crowley as a writer on a level with Joyce and D H Lawrence. His biographer Hutchison says this was only because they were unaware of his scandalous personal life.

His Heritage

There are different levels on which he is appreciated and understood. He has his followers who take Aiwass literally as the herald of the new Aeon.

There are many more who enjoy reading about his life because it entertains, amuses and inspires.

There have been a number of Crowley centred discussion groups on the Internet, some of which survive.

There is an Aleister Crowley Society. Much discussion is of an intellectually high standard.

Sympathetic readers discover such startling originality as to make all modern thought tedious variations on a few well-worn themes. Not everyone is sympathetic. You either get him or you don't.

About the Authors

John S Moore is a freelance writer and independent scholar living in London. He is the author of *Aleister Crowley: A Modern Master* (Mandrake of Oxford, 2009) and *Nietzsche - An Interpretation*, (AuthorsOnline Ltd, 2011) and has written on Schopenhauer, Wittgenstein and Edward Bulwer-

Lytton among others. More information at www.johnsmoore.co.uk

John Patrick Higgins is a writer and illustrator. He is the author of *The Narwhal and Other stories*. His second collection will be published later in the year. He writes art criticism for various magazines and is Creative Director of Shot Glass Theatre Company. He lives in Belfast, which he continues to find extraordinary.

Bibliography

Some Books by Aleister Crowley

Magick in Theory and Practice, New York: Dover, 1976.

The Book of Lies, Ilfracombe: Haydn Press, 1962.

Liber Aleph, or the Book of Wisdom or Folly, West Point, Cal.: Thelema Publishing Co., 1962.

The Confessions, London: Routledge and Kegan Paul, 1979.

The Holy Books of Thelema, New York, 1989.

Magick without Tears, St. Paul: Llewellyn Publications, 1973.

The Magical Record of the Beast 666: the diaries of Aleister Crowley, 1914-1920. edited Symonds and Grant, London: Duckworth, 1972.

Collected works of Aleister Crowley, Des Plaines: Yogi Publication Society, 1974.

The Law is for All, Phoenix: Falcon Press, 1985.

A Vindication of Nietzsche, Kokopeli Publishing, 1996.

Moonchild, New York: Samuel Weiser, 1970.

Konx Om Pax, London: Walter Scott Publishing, 1907.

The Compete Astrological Writings, London: Duckworth, 1974.

Songs for Italy, London: Neptune Press (no date).

Crowley on Christ, London: C.W. Daniel, 1974.

Some Books about Crowley

Martin Booth - *A Magick Life: The Biography of Aleister Crowley*, London: Hodder & Stoughton, 2000.

Charles R. Cammell - *Aleister Crowley, the Man: the Mage: the Poet*, London: Richards Press, 1951.

John F. C. Fuller - *The Star in the West, a critical essay upon the works of Aleister Crowley*, London & Felling-on-Tyne: Walter Scott Publishing Co, 1907.

Roger Hutchinson - *Aleister Crowley:The Beast Demystified*: Mainstream, 1998.

Arthur Calder Marshall - *The Magic of my Youth*, London: Rupert Hart-Davis, 1951.

Francis King - *The Magical World Of Aleister Crowley*, London: Weidenfeld and Nicolson, 1977.

P T Mistlberger - *The Three Dangerous Magi: Osho, Gurdjieff, Crowley*, Ropley: Axis Mundi Books, 2010.

John Moore - *Aleister Crowley: a Modern Master*, Oxford: Mandrake, 2009.

Pasi Marco - *Aleister Crowley and the Temptation of Politics*: Acumen, 2014 (translated from the Italian of 1999).

Israel Regardie - *The Eye in the Triangle, An interpretation of Aleister Crowley*, St. Paul, Minn.: Llewellyn Publications, 1970.

Susan Roberts - *The Magician of the Golden Dawn*, Chicago: Contemporary Books, 1978.

Richard B Spence - *Secret Agent 666, Aleister Crowley, British Intelligence and the Occult*, Los Angeles: Feral House, 2008.

Percy R Stephensen - *The Legend of Aleister Crowley*, London: Mandrake Press, 1930.

Gerald Suster - *The Legacy of the Beast*, London: W H Allen, 1988.

Lawrence Sutin - *Do what thou wilt : a Life of Aleister Crowley*, New York, 2002.

John Symonds - *The Great Beast*, London: Rider, 1951.

John Symonds - *The King of the Shadow Realm*, London: Duckworth, 1989.

You might also enjoy these titles:

Aleister Crowley :
A Modern Master -
By John Moore

ISBN 978-1-906958-02-2, £10.99, 216pp

Aleister Crowley's appeal on the level of popular culture has been well catered for by a number of biographies that have appeared in recent years, but the more intellectual side to him, which is equally fascinating, has not received so much serious treatment. Crowley, a Modern Master is neither an account of his life, nor a straightforward presentation of his teaching, but an attempt to place him clearly in the context of modern ideas as well as a number of older traditions.

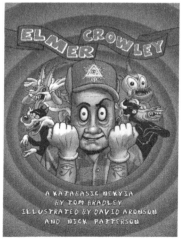

Elmer Crowley
a katabasic nekyia
Tom Bradley
(illustrated by David Aronson &
Nick Patterson - many in colour)

ISBN 978-1-906958-55-8, $17.99/£10, 132pp

Bless me,

curse me. For better or worse, my fallopian fall into matter. . .

After making careful preparations to ensure himself a proper reincarnation, the dying ALEISTER CROWLEY flubs one syllable of the magickal incantation . . .

and comes back as ELMER FUDD.

Lightning Source UK Ltd.
Milton Keynes UK
UKOW06f0919291215

265472UK00019B/887/P